English Unlimited

A2 Elementary B
Coursebook

Alex Tilbury, Theresa Clementson, Leslie Anne Hendra & David Rea
Course consultant: Adrian Doff

CAMBRIDGE
UNIVERSITY PRESS

CAMBRIDGE UNIVERSITY PRESS
Cambridge, New York, Melbourne, Madrid, Cape Town,
Singapore, São Paulo, Delhi, Mexico City

Cambridge University Press
Insurgentes Sur 1196, piso 10, Mexico, D.F., Mexico

www.cambridge-la.org

English Unlimited Split Combo Edition © Cambridge University Press 2013
Adapted from English Unlimited © Cambridge University Press 2010

English Unlimited Split Combo Edition first published 2013

Printed in Peru by Empressa Editora El Comercio S.A.

ISBN 978-1-107-64928-6 Elementary Combo B Coursebook with e-Portfolio and
                       Self-study Pack (Workbook with DVD-ROM)
ISBN 978-1-107-69183-4 Elementary Teacher's Pack
ISBN 978-0-521-69775-0 Elementary Class Audio CDs

How to use this coursebook

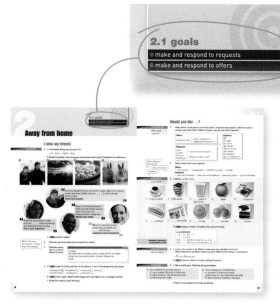

Every unit of this book is divided into sections, with clear, practical **goals** for learning. The 'R' pages to which students are directed comprise sections of activities and reference materials that follow after the units.

The first four pages of the unit help you build your language skills and knowledge. These pages include speaking, listening, reading, writing, grammar, vocabulary and pronunciation activities. They are followed by a **Target activity** which will help you put together what you have learned.

The **Explore** section of the unit begins with a **Keyword**, which looks at one of the most common and useful words in English. It also includes either an **Across cultures** or an **Independent learning** section, and then an **Explore speaking** or **Explore writing** task. The Explore section gives you extra language and skills work, all aiming to help you become a better communicator in English and a more effective learner.

The **Look again** section takes another look at the target language for the unit, helping you to review and extend your learning.
Sometimes you will also find this recycling symbol with the goals, to show when a particular goal is not new but is recycling language that you have met before.

This symbol shows you when you can hear and practise the correct pronunciation of key language, using the audio CD.

The **e-Portfolio** DVD-ROM contains useful reference material for all the units, as well as self-assessment to help you test your own learning, and Wordcards to help you test your vocabulary learning.

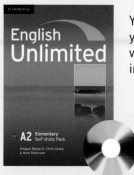

You can do more practice by yourself using the **Self-study Pack**, which includes a workbook and interactive DVD-ROM.

The DVD-ROM contains video and over 300 interactive activities.

Contents

Contents

8

What's she like?

8.1 goals
◎ talk about your family
◎ describe people's personality

Family

VOCABULARY
Family

Vocabulary reference
Family, R-12

1 **a** Which of these family members are male? Which are female? Which can be either?

aunt   brother   child   children   cousin   daughter   father/dad
grandfather   grandmother   mother/mum   niece   nephew
parents   sister   son   twins   uncle

b 🎧 **2.35** Listen to check. ⓟ

LISTENING

2 🎧 **2.36** Listen to Onyinye talking about her family. Match questions 1–3 with parts A–C of the conversation.

1   How many people are there in your family? ☐
2   Who are you closest to? ☐
3   Where does your family live? ☐

3 **a** Can you complete Onyinye's sentences?

1   I have four _____ .
2   Most of my family live in _____ .
3   My uncle and aunt have _____ children, or eight children.
4   I live with my _____ , so I see her a lot of the time.
5   I see my _____ quite often.
6   The member of my family that I'm closest to is my _____ .
7   We _____ very similar and we have similar style.

b 🎧 **2.36** Listen again to check.

4 Do you think Onyinye has a large family? Think about families you know.

PRONUNCIATION
The schwa
sound 2

5 **a** Words or syllables without stress often have a schwa /ə/ sound. Can you find six more /ə/ sounds in these expressions?

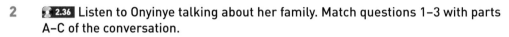

most of my family   a lot of the time
another part of England   a member of my family

b 🎧 **2.37** Listen and read the script on R-14 to check. ⓟ Practise saying the expressions.

SPEAKING

6 **a** Look again at the questions in 2 and think about your own answers.

b Tell each other about your families.

Friends

READING

1 Read the information about two friends. How do you think they met?

ED SMITH was born in England in 1977, the son of the novelist and teacher Jonathan Smith. He went to Tonbridge School and Cambridge University, and is now a well-known cricketer and journalist.

Poet and novelist VIKRAM SETH was born in India in 1952. He went to schools in India and England, and studied at universities in England, the USA and China. His novels include A Suitable Boy and An Equal Music.

2 a In A/B pairs, read to check how Vikram and Ed met.
A, read Vikram's article on this page and answer questions 1–6.
B, read Ed's article on p126 and answer questions 1–6 there.

1 How old was Ed when Vikram met him?
2 Where did they meet?
3 Why did Vikram write a poem for Ed?
4 When and where did they meet for the second time?
5 What's Ed like? *He's outgoing and ...*
6 What does Vikram say about his friendship with Ed?

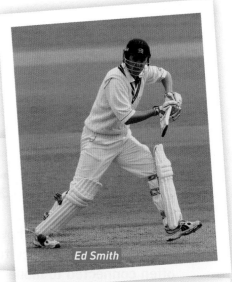
Ed Smith

How we met

VIKRAM SETH ON ED SMITH

I first met Ed when he was about sixteen. I was at his father's house but I don't remember much about Ed then – he was just the son of my old English teacher. His dad invited me to stay the night so I had Ed's room and I think Ed slept on the sofa. The next morning I wrote him a poem to say thank you.

Years later I was in Australia and I got a call saying, "Can I meet you? I'm Ed Smith, Jonathan Smith's son." And I said, "Of course you can." In India, if your friend's child phones up and asks if they can meet you, the answer is "yes", no question. So I couldn't say no and I'm happy I didn't. I like Ed and I admire him in many ways.

Ed is young and old at the same time. He's outgoing and adventurous and also very independent and hard-working. He wants to do his best in life. It's difficult to say why we're friends. We don't ask a lot of each other, we just enjoy our friendship. Whenever I meet him it's interesting.

Vikram Seth

b Tell each other about your articles. Find out two new things about Ed and Vikram's friendship.

VOCABULARY
Personality

3 a Tick the adjectives you know from the articles about Ed and Vikram. Then check the meanings in a dictionary or on R-12.

> adventurous   creative   funny   hard-working
> independent   intelligent   outgoing   serious

b 🔊 **2.38** Practise saying the words. **P**

SPEAKING

4 a Write the names of five people in your life: friends, family or colleagues. What are they like? Use personality adjectives from 3a.

b Show each other your names. Ask questions to find out about the people.

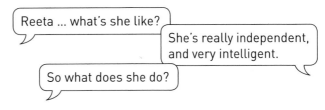

Reeta ... what's she like?

She's really independent, and very intelligent.

So what does she do?

Fashion sense

READING

1 Find these things in pictures A–C.

1 a wig
2 jewels
3 a beauty spot
4 a necklace
5 make-up

2 Read the guide to an exhibition on the history of fashion. Which part, 1 or 2, talks about:

1 fashions today?
2 fashions in the past?
3 clothes?
4 hairstyles?
5 skin?

CHANGING IMAGE

This exhibition shows how ideas of beauty and fashion change with culture and time and are often connected to money, beliefs and lifestyle.

1 In 1624, King Louis XIII of France started wearing a wig because he was bald. Soon fashionable men in Northern Europe started wearing wigs, like the man in this picture. Under the wig, his hair is shaved or tied back.

This 18th-century woman has got a large white wig with jewels in it. She is wearing white make-up and has got a black beauty spot to show her pale skin. Pale skin was fashionable for hundreds of years in Northern Europe because it showed that you didn't work outside in the fields. Then, in 1923, fashion designer Coco Chanel came back from holiday with a tan. Suddenly a tan showed you had a lot of money and could travel to hot countries. By the 1970s, tans were very popular in Europe.

2 Today, Indian fashions change from place to place. This woman is wearing a *sari*, the traditional dress of Indian women. The type of sari often shows a woman's age, occupation and religion and where she comes from. She's got a special necklace to show that she's married, and a red dot on her forehead, often called a *bindi*. Traditionally, the bindi also shows that someone is married, but nowadays a lot of unmarried women and even children have bindis because they are fashionable.

Most Indian women wear traditional dress but men in towns and cities in all regions of India usually wear western-style clothing, like shirts and trousers. In villages, however, many men are still more comfortable in traditional clothing.

3 Read again and answer the questions.

1 Why did people in Northern Europe want to wear wigs? have pale skin? have a tan?
2 What can a *sari* often show about the person who wears it? What about a *bindi*?
3 What's the difference between the way women and men dress in India?

SPEAKING

4 Talk in groups.

1 What current fashions do you like? What fashions do you dislike?
2 What colours and styles suit you?
3 Do you wear special clothes for special occasions? What?
4 Do you like make-up, or jewellery?
5 Do you think the things people wear show their personality? What else can they show?

VOCABULARY
Appearance

5 Which of these words can you use to describe the people in the exhibition guide? What about people in your class?

She's / He's	very tall short medium height beautiful bald
She's / He's wearing	make-up jewellery glasses high heels trousers a jacket a dress
She's / He's got	long / short hair blue / brown / green eyes dark / pale skin a tan a beard a moustache glasses

WRITING

She's a singer.
She's very beautiful.
She's got long black hair.

6 a Think of a famous person in your country or around the world. Write a description.

He's an ...   He's very ...   He usually wears ...   He's got ...

b Listen to each other's descriptions. Guess who the people are.

He's got a beard

GRAMMAR
have got

1 a In these sentences, *have got* means the same as *have*.

They **have got** pale skin. = They **have** pale skin.
She **has got** a special necklace. = She **has** a special necklace.

Complete the sentences in the box with the correct form of have got.

I / you / we / they	he / she / it
1 ❓ _____ you got glasses? 2 ✅❌ Yes, I have. / No, I haven't. 3 ➕ They've got pale skin. 4 ➖ I _____ _____ a lot of jewellery.	5 ❓ _____ she got a tan? 6 ✅❌ Yes, she has. / No, she hasn't. 7 ➕ She _____ _____ a *bindi*. 8 ➖ He _____ _____ a beard or moustache.
In conversation, use the short forms: have got > 've got has got > 's got	

b 🔊 2.39 Listen to check. ℗

2 Complete this paragraph about another picture in the exhibition. Use the correct form of have got.

In the mid-1800s in Northern Europe, it was important for people to look clean and tidy.
In this picture of a British couple, they aren't wearing wigs and they ¹_____ plain and simple clothes. The man ²_____ short hair, a beard and a moustache. The woman ³_____ long hair, tied back, and she ⁴_____ any make-up. They ⁵_____ any jewellery.

Grammar reference and practice, p138

SPEAKING

3 Choose a picture on R-2. Take turns to describe a person. Listen and guess which picture it is.

I think this is in the 1970s, probably in Europe.

4 a Look at all the pictures together. Guess where the people are from and when they lived.

b Check your ideas on R-4.

8.3 Target activity

Describe someone you admire

8.3 goals

- describe people's personality
- describe people's appearance
- describe relationships

TASK LISTENING

1 🔊 **2.40** Listen to Lesley talking about someone she admires. Which person in photos 1–5 does she talk about?

2 a 🔊 **2.40** Listen again. What does Lesley say about Sybil? Circle the correct words.

1   She's a relative / a neighbour.
2   She loves going out / talking.
3   She wants to live alone / with her daughter.
4   She's happy / not happy with her home and her life.
5   Her father / uncle trained her for a car race.
6   She won the race and still has the silver car / cup.

b Read the script on R-14 to check.

TASK VOCABULARY

Relationships

3 a Look at sentences a–i. Which is about:

1   how often you see or contact each other?
2   how close your relationship is?
3   how similar your interests are?

a   We don't see each other a lot.
b   We get on really well.
c   We're interested in the same things.
d   We can talk about everything together.
e   We get in touch maybe twice a year.
f   We like different things.
g   We spend a lot of time together.
h   We're very close.
i   We don't know each other very well.

b 🔊 **2.41** Listen to check. ℗

TASK

4 a Plan a short description of someone you admire. Think about these questions.

1   How did you meet?
2   What kind of relationship do you have?
3   What's he/she like?
4   What does he/she look like?
5   Why do you admire him/her?

> OK, a person I really admire is my friend Kenji. I first met him at ...

b In groups, tell each other about the people. Ask some questions to find out more.

Keyword *like*

1 **a** Look at sentences A–D from previous units. Then add *like* to sentences 1–8.

> A I like Ed and I admire him in many ways. Unit 8
> B I'd like to go to Cuba and Ireland. Unit 2 **(= want)**
> C Our mum says we're like twins, just born ten years apart. Unit 8 **(= are similar to)**
> D Soon fashionable men ... started wearing wigs, like the man in this picture. Unit 8 **(= for example)**

like
1 Would you ⋀ anything from home? Unit 2
2 I don't bad news. Unit 3
3 We all play yunnori. It's chess. Unit 3
4 There are more and more people José Luis all over the world. Unit 5
5 How many would you? Unit 6
6 But sometimes I do extra work, writing reviews. Unit 7
7 I going to bed late. Unit 7
8 Men in towns and cities in all regions of India usually wear western-style clothing, shirts and trousers. Unit 8

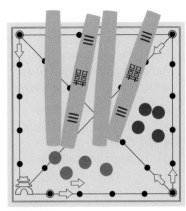

yunnori

b Are sentences 1–8 like sentences A, B, C or D?

2 **a** Complete the sentences with your own ideas.

1 I'm like my .... We're both ...
2 I like going ...
3 I usually wear ... , like ...
4 I'd like to buy ...

I usually wear smart clothes to work, like a jacket and tie.

b Listen to each other's sentences. Ask questions to find out more.

Independent learning Reading the phonemic script 1: consonants

1 **a** You can use the *Sounds of English* chart on p160 to help you with the pronunciation of new words. Match the symbols 1–8 with the sounds in these words.

> **adventurous** /əd'ventʃərəs/ *adj*
> liking to try new or difficult things:
> *I'm going to be more adventurous with my cooking.*
>
> *Cambridge Essential English Dictionary*

short ☐ outgoing ☐ children ☐ usually ☐ brother ☐
jewellery ☐ thanks [1] yellow ☐

p	t	k	f	θ¹	s	ʃ³	tʃ⁵
b	d	g	v	ð²	z	ʒ⁴	dʒ⁶
h	l	m	n	ŋ⁷	r	j⁸	w

b ▶ 2.42 Listen to check.

2 Complete the pronunciation of these words. Use the consonant symbols.

big /_ɪ_/   listen /'_ɪ_ə_/   forest /'_ɒ_ɪ__/   colleague /_ɒ__iː_/   job /_ɒ_/
kitchen /'_ɪ_ɪ_/   reading /'_iː_ɪ_/   passport /_ɑː___ɔː_/   maths /_æ__/

3 **a** Can you read these words from units 0–8? How do you say them?

/'ælfəbet/   /bɪ'kɒz/   /nekst/   /'ɒfɪs/   /tə'geðə/

b ▶ 2.43 Listen to check.

4 **a** Find out how to say these words from unit 8. Use a dictionary, or check on R-13.

necklace exhibition traditional image fashionable

b ▶ 2.44 Listen to check.

8 EXPLOREWriting

1 How many people in the class are:

1 first-born children?
2 middle children?
3 last-born children?
4 only children?

2 Read the website article. According to Michael Grose, which children are usually:

a artistic and creative?
b ambitious and serious?
c confident?
d relaxed and outgoing?

3 Read four web postings about the article. Who agrees with Michael Grose? Who disagrees?

MEDIAWATCH

First borns 'are more ambitious'

First-born children are more ambitious than their brothers and sisters, says parenting expert Michael Grose in his new book *Why first-borns rule the world and last-borns want to change it*. First-borns are serious and hard-working and many become lawyers or doctors. He says only children are similar to first borns. They are confident but need to learn to share with other people. Middle children are relaxed and outgoing, have more friends and are good at meeting new people. Last-born children are often artistic and creative but need to learn to take responsibility. He believes a child's position in the family is connected to personality, behaviour, learning and work.

Your comments

W Chen, Hong Kong
Today, 12.25 pm
I agree with Michael Grose. Here, first-born children have to look after younger brothers and sisters so they're usually more serious. The last-borns are more creative because they can do what they want. Middle children need to be good with people because they're less popular than the 'important' first child and 'special' last child!

Erika, Ljubljana
Today, 11.46 am
I don't agree with the writer. I think the important thing is that our brothers and sisters are happy and we look after each other. We all need to learn to share and be responsible for ourselves and help other people. Your position in the family isn't important.

Sapna, Mumbai
Today, 9.15 am
Personally, I think Michael Grose is right. I was the first-born child so I had to work hard to help our family when we had problems. My younger brother didn't do anything! My parents said he was too small.

Eduardo Lopez, Mexico City
Yesterday, 10.02 pm
I'm the fifth of six children so what about me? Am I a 'middle child'? My eldest brother's a writer, I'm an architect and have my own company and my youngest sister's a very good doctor. I agree with some of Grose's ideas, but I don't think the job you get is connected to birth order. You can't become a lawyer or doctor if your family's too poor to pay for the education and training.

---

4 a *so* Cover the web page. Add so to the sentences below.

1 Here, first-born children have to look after younger brothers and sisters they're usually more serious.
2 I'm the fifth of six children what about me?
3 I was the first-born child I had to work hard to help our family when we had problems.

b Look at the web page to check your answers.

5 Complete the expressions for giving opinions.

1 I _____ with Michael Grose.
2 I don't agree _____ the writer.
3 I _____ the important thing is that ...
4 _____ , I think Michael Grose is right.
5 I agree with some of Grose's ideas, _____ I _____ think ...

6 a Write a web posting giving your opinion about the article. Use expressions from 4 and 5.

b Read other students' web postings. Do you agree with each other?

8 Look again ♻

Review

VOCABULARY Appearance

1 **a** Complete the profile of Nicky on a social networking website. Use *be* or *have got* in the correct form.

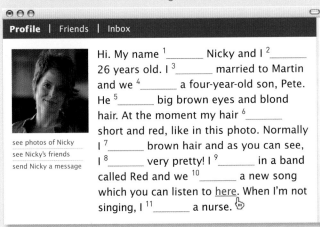

Profile | Friends | Inbox

see photos of Nicky
see Nicky's friends
send Nicky a message

Hi. My name ¹_____ Nicky and I ²_____ 26 years old. I ³_____ married to Martin and we ⁴_____ a four-year-old son, Pete. He ⁵_____ big brown eyes and blond hair. At the moment my hair ⁶_____ short and red, like in this photo. Normally I ⁷_____ brown hair and as you can see, I ⁸_____ very pretty! I ⁹_____ in a band called Red and we ¹⁰_____ a new song which you can listen to <u>here</u>. When I'm not singing, I ¹¹_____ a nurse.

b Write a profile of yourself for a website. Think about:

- family • appearance • personality
- work • free time • other interesting facts

c Read each other's profiles. Find out three new things about each person.

GRAMMAR *have got*

2 **a** Write a list of five of your favourite possessions.

my car, my iPod, my bed, my music collection …

b Look at another student's list. Write one or two questions with *have got* about each possession.

What kind of … have you got? Has it got a …? How many … has it got?

c Ask and answer your questions in pairs.

CAN YOU REMEMBER? Unit 7 – Work and studies

3 **a** Complete the questions with the correct prepositions.

| at (x2)   in   for   on (x2)   to |

1   What was your favourite subject _____ school?
2   Do you work _____ an office?
3   Do you ever go _____ business trips?
4   Do you often work _____ home?
5   Who do you work _____?
6   What are you working _____ at the moment?
7   How often do you go _____ meetings or conferences?

b Write two more questions to ask another student about work or studies.

c Ask and answer the questions in pairs.

Extension

SPELLING AND SOUNDS *ee, ea, ie*

4 **a** ▶ 2.45 Listen to these words from unit 8. Notice the different spellings of /iː/.

agree   teacher   niece

b Work in pairs. Complete these words with *ee, ea* or *ie*.

1   He always wears j_ _ns.
2   How did you m_ _t?
3   I don't bel_ _ve you.
4   I don't eat m_ _t.
5   I've got thr_ _ children.
6   I love r_ _ding.
7   She's got gr_ _n eyes.
8   We don't see _ _ch other often.
9   I like working in a t_ _m.
10 Are you fr_ _ tonight?

c ▶ 2.46 Spellcheck. Close your book. Listen to ten words and write them down.

d Check your spelling.

NOTICE *to* for giving reasons

5 **a** Make three sentences. Then check in the articles on p68 and R-2.

1   He visited Tonbridge
2   She's got a black beauty spot
3   She's got a special necklace

a   to show that she's married.
b   to give a reading.
c   to show her pale skin.

b Change the <u>underlined</u> words so the sentences are true for you.

1   I'm learning English <u>to get a good job</u>.
    I'm learning English to travel.
2   I use the internet <u>to buy music</u>.
3   I go to the city centre <u>to meet my friends</u>.
4   <u>To keep fit</u>, I go swimming every weekend.
5   <u>To relax</u>, I watch TV.

c Compare your sentences in groups.

Getting around

How do you get there?

VOCABULARY
Using transport

Vijay from London, England

1 Match the questions with Vijay's answers a–e.

1 How do you get to the city centre?
2 How do you get to the shops?
3 How do you usually get to work?
4 How do you get to your closest friend's home?
5 How do you get to the airport?

a Well, it's a bit difficult to get there by public transport, so I usually walk. He rides a motorbike and that's how he gets to my place.

b Well, I usually get the underground because it's cheaper. But if it's a business trip, I get a taxi.

c I drive because I usually buy more than I can carry.

d I get the train. I hate driving on crowded roads and it's difficult to park in the centre.

e I cycle most days but if I'm late, I get the bus.

2 a Match the highlighted verbs and expressions with pictures 1–8.

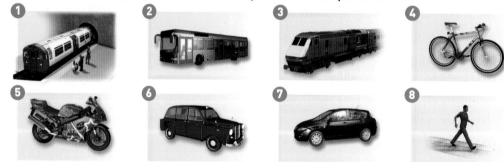

b 🔊 **2.47** Listen to check. **℗**

c What other kinds of transport do you know? *scooter, the Metro*

SPEAKING

3 In groups, ask and answer the questions in 1. Find out who:

1 walks the most.
2 drives the most.
3 uses public transport the most.
4 cycles the most.

A visitor in Lucknow

LISTENING

Vijay is visiting his cousin Meera in Lucknow, India.

1 🔊 **2.48** Listen to Vijay talking to Meera. Is this his first visit to Lucknow?

2 a 🔊 **2.49** Listen again. Are these sentences true or false?

1 There are cash machines near Meera's house.
2 Vijay wants to buy an English book.
3 Universal Booksellers opens very early.
4 It takes about twenty minutes to walk to the centre of Lucknow.
5 Meera and Vijay decide to walk to the city centre.

b Read the script on R-14 to check your answers.

an auto-rickshaw or 'auto'

VOCABULARY

Getting information

3 **a** Complete the questions from Meera and Vijay's conversation with these words.

> best   know   near   nearest   take   can

Asking where something is

Is there a cash machine _____ here?

Are there any bookshops here?

Where's the _____ rickshaw stop?

Asking how to get there

What's the _____ way to get there?

_____ we walk?

Is there a bus?

Asking how far away it is

How long does it _____?

Asking when it's open

Do you _____ when it's open?

b Add these questions to the correct groups in 3a.

> Is it far?   What time does it open?
> Where can I buy some shoes?
> How far is it?

4 **a** Complete the questions in the conversations.

1
A Where's the nearest bus stop?
B It's on Station Road.
A What's _____?
B Oh, you can walk.
A How _____?
B About half a kilometre.

2
A Is _____ a bank _____?
B Not really. The nearest one is next to the train station.
A Is _____?
B It's better to get the metro.
A How _____?
B About fifteen minutes.

3
A Where _____?
B The best shoe shop is Porter's.
A Is _____?
B No. It's a ten-minute walk.
A What _____?
B It opens at nine-thirty.

b **2.49** Listen to check.

PRONUNCIATION

Sentence stress and /ə/

5 **a** Underline the stressed syllables in 4a, conversation 1. Then mark the schwa sounds with /ə/.

A _Where's_ the _nearest_ _bus_ stop?

b Look at the script on R-14 to check. **P** Practise saying the conversation in pairs.

6 Practise all the conversations in 4a, changing the highlighted words.

> Where's the nearest cinema?
> It's on 127th Street.

SPEAKING

7 **a** Think of three places you might need to find when you're visiting a new place. For example:

• a bank   • a post office   • a supermarket   • gift shops
• a hotel   • the tourist information office   • a train station

> Excuse me. Where's the nearest train station?
> It's on Park Street.

b You leave the building you're in now. Stop another student to ask for information.

c Ask your questions again to another student. Are the answers the same?

King of the road

READING

1 a Look at the picture of Joe Marshall.
Why do you think he rides a unicycle to work?

1 He enjoys it.
2 It's quick and safe.
3 He likes people looking at him.
4 It's good exercise.
5 It's good in traffic jams.
6 It's cheap.

b Read the article to check your ideas.

One-wheeled wonder

The unicycle is the real king of the road

Forget public transport. For computer programmer Joe Marshall, the daily journey to work across one of the most crowded cities in the world is fun. "It's like playing on the way to work," he says.

It takes Joe 50 minutes to travel the nine-mile journey across London by unicycle. That's about the same as it takes on the bus or the underground, and ten minutes quicker than by car. "Unicycles are slower than bikes," he says, "but they're the best thing in traffic jams because you can turn in a really small space. It's great exercise, too, because you can't stop moving. I have to jump up and down at traffic lights."

But aren't unicycles more dangerous than bikes? Marshall doesn't think so. "Unicycles are safer than they look and easier to ride," he says. "And drivers are more careful with me than with cyclists." Long-distance unicycling is more common than many people think. "Someone rode across America a few years ago," Marshall says. "That's the longest trip ever on a unicycle. And last year a group of people rode across Norway."

But what about all the looks you get? "You can't worry about what people think," he says. "Most of them are all right but I get a lot of comments, like 'Where's the other wheel?' A few days ago, an old lady came up to me and said, 'That's really stupid. Buy a car!'"

2 Read the article again. Who thinks unicycles are fun? dangerous? stupid?

3 What do you think of Joe's form of transport?

Comparing

GRAMMAR

Comparatives
and superlatives

1 Read the second paragraph again and answer the questions.

To get across London, what's:
1 **quicker** than a unicycle?
2 **slower** than a unicycle?
3 **the best** form of transport when there's a lot of traffic?

2 a Complete the table with comparative and superlative adjectives from the article.

	comparative	superlative
1 syllable quick safe long	+er _____ _____ longer	+est the quickest the safest the _____
2 syllables or more careful crowded dangerous	more ... _____ more crowded _____	the most ... the most careful the _____ the most dangerous
2 syllables -y easy	+ier _____	+iest the easiest
irregular good bad far	better worse further	the _____ the worst the furthest

b 🔊 **2.50** Listen to check. 🅟

c What are the comparative and superlative forms of these adjectives? Use the table to help you.

cheap   busy   clean   expensive   interesting   nice   comfortable

3 Practise conversations 1–5 in pairs. Then use the adjectives in brackets to change the conversations.

1
A How can I get into town?
B Well, you could get a bus but it's easier to walk. (interesting, nice)

2
A I think I'll get a taxi to the airport.
B Well, the subway's quicker than a taxi. (cheap)

3
A What's the quickest way to get to the shopping centre? (easy)
B The underground. It only takes 10 minutes.

4
A Do you always cycle to work?
B Yes. It's the cheapest way to get there. (nice, best)

5
A How do I get to the train station?
B The best way is to get the bus. (quick, comfortable)

Grammar reference and practice, R-7

Journeys

VOCABULARY

Prepositions of movement

1 Read Jaynie's description of a journey she likes.

❝One of my favourite journeys is walking ¹from my house in Lower Sydenham ²to the shopping area in Lewisham. I go ³out of my front door and ⁴across Southend Lane and then, after a few minutes, I go ⁵down some steps and ⁶into a quiet, riverside park. It's really beautiful, with lots of trees, flowers and green grass. I walk for about forty minutes near the river and then go ⁷through Ladywell Fields, a large park. Then I go ⁸up some steps and right at the top is Bardsley's, my favourite café, and some nice shops.❞

2 Match the prepositions in Jaynie's description with pictures A–H.

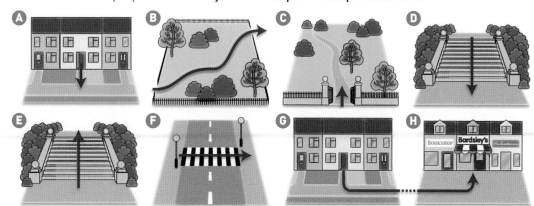

WRITING AND SPEAKING

3 Write a short description of a journey you like.

4 Listen to each other's journeys. Which do you think is the most interesting?

Buy a ticket

9.3 goals
- get information in places you visit
- compare ways of travelling
- buy a travel ticket

TASK LISTENING

1   Vijay wants to visit a friend at his new house in Basingstoke, England. Look at his coach ticket.

EXPRESSCoach

PASSENGER TICKET

From: London Victoria
To: Basingstoke
Type: OPEN RETURN
Service: 022
19 May
Adult: 01   Child: 00

Total Fare: £15.45

1   Where's he travelling from?
2   Where's he going?
3   Is it a single or a return ticket?
4   What's the departure date?
5   How much did the ticket cost?

2   **2.51** Listen to Vijay buying his ticket. Circle the correct words.

1   He wants to go to Basingstoke today / tomorrow.
2   With a day return ticket, he comes back today / tomorrow.
3   With an open return, he can come back any time / at the weekend.
4   The day return is more expensive / cheaper.
5   The 4.15 coach is faster / slower than the 4.30 coach.

TASK VOCABULARY

Buying a ticket

3   **a**   Match the questions and answers.

1   How much does an open return ticket cost?
2   What time does the next coach leave?
3   Is it direct?
4   How long does it take to Basingstoke?
5   Which coach do I get?
6   Where do I get it?

a   The direct coach? About an hour and a half.
b   Number 342.
c   It leaves at 4.15, in fifteen minutes.
d   To Basingstoke? It's £15.45.
e   Just outside those doors. You'll see the sign.
f   No. You need to change coaches once.

b   **2.51** Listen again to check.

c   Use these words to make five new questions using the highlighted expressions in 3a.

bus   a single   train   a day return   Birmingham

TASK

4   **a**   You want to buy a ticket. Work in A/B pairs. A, read your role cards on R-3. B, read your role cards on R-5.

b   Think of questions to ask about prices, times and other travel details.

5   **a**   Take turns to buy a ticket. Have conversation 1 first, then conversation 2.

b   Change role cards and have two more conversations.

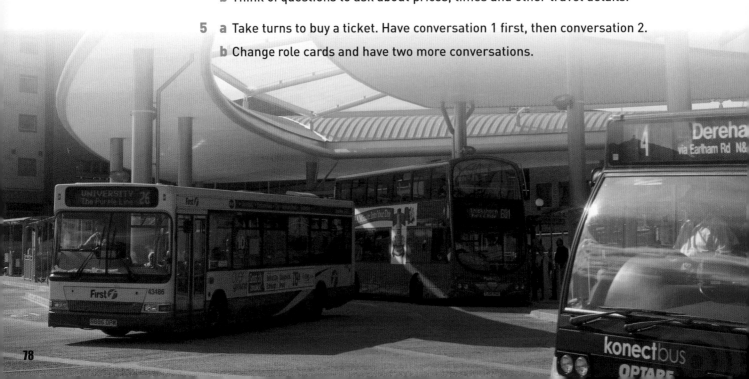

Keyword *get*

get = *receive, obtain, buy*

1   Get with a noun usually means *receive*, *obtain* or *buy*. Complete the sentences from previous units with these words.

job   dollars   newspapers
comments   salary   calls

> 1 I get a lot of _____, like 'Where's the other wheel?' 2   How many phone _____ do you usually get every day?
> 3 I get my _____ at the end of the month.
> 4 Did you get some US _____ for me?
> 5 I want to get a good _____ and learn salsa.
> 6 Can you get some _____ ?

2   Ask and answer the questions.

1   How many emails, texts and phone calls do you get every day?
2   How often do you get magazines or newspapers?
3   How much holiday do you get every year?
4   What presents did you get for your last birthday?
5   Where's the best place to get a good cup of coffee near you?

get = *travel, arrive*

3   In which sentences does get mean *arrive*?
In which sentences does it mean *travel on*?

> 1 You can get the number forty-three bus.
> 2 Can we talk when I get home?
> 3 I usually get the underground because it's cheaper.
> 4 It's a bit difficult to get there by public transport.

4   Talk in pairs. How do you get to:

* your doctor?
* your hairdresser?
* your nearest cinema?
* your workplace?
* your favourite café or restaurant?

5   What's the first thing you do when you:

* get to work?
* get home after work?

Across cultures Transport culture

1   a Which cities do you think the pictures show?

b 🔊 **2.52** Listen to Marike and Hasan talking about their cities and check your ideas.

2   a What do Marike and Hasan say about these things?

1	the government	3	the price of petrol	5	roads
2	traffic lights	4	taxis	6	bike lanes

b 🔊 **2.52** Listen again to check.

3   Match 1–6 with a–f. Which sentences are about which cities?

1   We don't have a big   a   bike lanes and bike traffic lights.
2   The city has   b   bicycles first and cars second.
3   Everyone I know   c   bicycle-friendly.
4   The government thinks about   d   car culture.
5   We're really   e   uses a car.
6   People really   f   love their cars.

4   In groups, discuss the questions.

1   Do you think you live in a car culture, a bike culture, or a public transport culture?
2   Does your town or city have bike lanes? What's the public transport like?
3   What forms of transport do most people use where you live?
4   Was it different ten years ago? What about twenty years ago?
5   Do you prefer private transport or public transport? Why?
6   Do you know any places with a very different 'transport culture' from where you live?

1 **2.53** Listen to the first part of Vijay and Sara's conversation. Answer the questions.

1 What day are they meeting?
2 What do they decide to do?

2 **2.54** Listen to the rest of the conversation. What time will they meet, and where?

3 **a** Look at the highlighted expressions in the conversation. Which expressions are for:

1 checking information?
2 correcting yourself?
3 correcting other people?
4 summarising information?

b What are these expressions for? Match them with 1–4 in 3a.

> So, just to repeat, …
> Sorry, I'm wrong. It's …
> No, it's …
> Do you mean …?

4 **a** **2.55** Listen. Which two words in each line have the strongest stress?

1 Was that Campie Street? P for Peter?
2 No, Cambie Street. B for Bob.
3 Sorry, not the Palace Theatre. I mean the Royal Theatre.
4 Sorry, is that 393 or 353?
5 Well, it's not next to the theatre, exactly. It's near it.

b Look at the script on R-15 to check. Practise saying the sentences. ℗

5 **a** You make a mistake and want to correct it. Add a correction after the first sentence, using the word in brackets.

1 Her name's Tracey <u>Clarence</u>. (Claremont)
   No, not Clarence. I mean Claremont.
2 The meeting's at the Hotel <u>Astoria</u>. (Astor)
3 Catch the number 42 bus and get off at <u>East</u> Broadway Station. (West)
4 His number's 356<u>332</u>. (342)

b Someone makes a mistake and you correct it. What do you say?

1 Is your name spelled <u>J-a-n-i-e</u>? (J-a-y-n-i-e)
   No, it's …
2 OK, see you on <u>Thursday</u> at 6.00. (Tuesday)
3 He's on Flight AC914 from <u>Ottawa</u>. (Toronto)
4 Is your surname <u>Walton</u>? W for west? (Malton)

Goals
- correct yourself and other people
- check and summarise information

> **VIJAY** …Well, there's a café in Cambie Street that has good food. I can't remember the name but it's really nice.
> **SARA** ¹Was that Campie Street? ²P for Peter?
> **VIJAY** ³No, Cambie Street. ⁴B for Bob … you know, it's where the Palace Theatre is. ⁵Sorry, not the Palace Theatre. I mean the Royal Theatre.
> **SARA** Oh, right. I know the Royal Theatre.
> **VIJAY** Well, the café's near the theatre. It has lots of big photos of actors on the walls.
> **SARA** It sounds interesting. Shall we meet at eight?
> **VIJAY** Yes, that's fine. Anyway, call me if you get lost. Do you have my mobile number?
> **SARA** I don't know. Tell me and I'll write it down.
> **VIJAY** OK, it's, er, 0791 334 4353.
> **SARA** ⁶Sorry, is that 393 or 353?
> **VIJAY** ⁷It's 353.
> **SARA** ⁸So, just to check, we're meeting at eight in the café next to the Royal Theatre, ⁹right?
> **VIJAY** ¹⁰Well, it's not next to the theatre, exactly. It's near it.
> **SARA** No problem. See you there.

6 Look at the information. In pairs, take turns to check the main points.

1 Next direct train for Basingstoke, leaves from Platform 2, 4.00

> So, just to check, the next direct train for Basingstoke leaves from Platform 2 at 4.00, right?

2 Bus number 15, goes to Central Station. Next one leaves 1.30
3 Open return ticket, £16.00, but day return ticket, £11.00
4 Party at Golden Lion Café, Fourth Avenue, near Green Park

7 **a** Work in pairs. A, look at the cards on R-3. B, look at the cards on R-5. Have two conversations.

b Change roles and repeat.

9 Look again ♻

Review

1 a Work in pairs. Write four forms of transport in a square.

b Take turns to compare them. For each comparison, draw a line. Try to use different adjectives.

OK, the bus is cheaper than a plane.

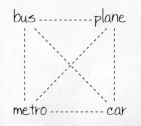

bus - - - - - - - - plane

metro - - - - - - - - car

c Choose a different topic and repeat.

- cities
- rooms
- activities
- films
- furniture
- food
- animals
- free time
- shops

GRAMMAR Superlatives

2 a Complete the sentences with the superlative form of the words.

1 What's *the best* restaurant you know? (good)
2 What's _____ way to travel? (dangerous)
3 What's _____ city you know? (crowded)
4 What's _____ car? (fast)
5 What's _____ shopping area? (busy)
6 What's _____ city to live in? (expensive)
7 What's _____ form of transport? (slow)
8 What's _____ free time activity? (boring)

b Ask and answer the questions. Express your opinions and give reasons.

I think The Golden Lion is the best restaurant.

Why?

Well, it has great food, like …

CAN YOU REMEMBER? Unit 8 – Personality adjectives

3 a Complete the personality adjectives with vowels.

```
_dv_nt_r__s          _nd_p_nd_nt
cr__t_v_             _nt_ll_g_nt
f_nny                _nt_r_st_ng
h_rd-w_rk_ng         s_r___s
```

b Think of one person for each adjective. The person can be from the past or present, someone you know or someone famous.

c Talk about the eight people in pairs.

My brother Henri is really adventurous. He likes mountain climbing and paragliding.

Extension

SPELLING AND SOUNDS Double consonants

4 a Which of these one-syllable words ends in *one* vowel + *one* consonant?

big   hot   quick   cheap

Now look at the comparative and superlative forms.

comparative	superlative
bigger, hotter *but* quicker, cheaper	biggest, hottest *but* quickest, cheapest

b How do you spell the comparative and superlative forms of these adjectives?

1 fat	3 old	5 long	7 safe
2 nice	4 wet	6 fit	8 fast

c You can use the same rule for other endings:

sun > sunny   stop > stopped
run > running   shop > shopping

d 🔊 **2.56** Spellcheck. Close your book. Listen to ten words and write them down.

e Check your spelling on R-15.

NOTICE *safer than it looks*

5 a Read the sentences. Do unicycles look safe or dangerous? Do many people think unicycling is common?

Unicycles are safer than they look.
Unicycling is more common than many people think.

b Complete the sentences with your own ideas.

1 … is easier than it looks.
2 … is safer than it looks.
3 … is more difficult than it looks.
4 … is more expensive than people think.
5 … is more interesting than people think.

c Compare sentences with a partner and explain your ideas.

Self-assessment

Can you do these things in English? Circle a number on each line. 1 = I can't do this, 5 = I can do this well.

◎ get information in places you visit	1	2	3	4	5
◎ compare ways of travelling	1	2	3	4	5
◎ buy a travel ticket	1	2	3	4	5
◎ correct yourself and other people	1	2	3	4	5
◎ check and summarise information	1	2	3	4	5

- For Wordcards, reference and saving your work → e-Portfolio
- For more practice → Self-study Pack, Unit 9

10 Getting together

10.1 goals

- talk about films
- find information in a cinema programme
- make and respond to suggestions

World cinema

VOCABULARY
Films

1 a 🎧 **3.1** Listen to eight short extracts from films. Match each extract with a kind of film.

> a documentary   a comedy   an action film   an animated film
> a drama   a science fiction film   a horror film   a romantic film

> Well, *Shrek*'s an animated film …

b Think of some examples of each kind of film.

c What kinds of film do you like? What kinds don't you like? Why?

READING

2 Read the cinema programme. What kind of film is on each day?

Monday: Annarth, an action film; Tuesday …

THE PICTURE HOUSE   International Film Week
See a selection of great films from around the world.

ANNARTH *India, 180 min, Mon 30 Oct, 7.00 pm*
A great action film. Sameer comes home to his village after ten long years and meets his old friend Jimmy (Sunil Shetty). Then Jimmy's brother kills Bandya, a member of a local criminal gang …

FAMILY LAW *(DERECHO DE FAMILIA) Argentina, 102 min, Tue 31 Oct, 7.30 pm*
Family Law is about the difficult relationship between a father and son, both lawyers in Buenos Aires. A comedy with a serious message. Excellent music by Cesar Lerner.

THE OTHERS *Spain, 100 min, Wed 1 Nov, 2.30 pm & 7.30 pm*
It is 1945, and Grace Stewart (Nicole Kidman) and her children live alone in a huge house. Strange things start to happen, and one of the children sees people no one else can see. Are Grace and her children really alone?

2 DAYS IN PARIS *France, 96 min, Thu 2 Nov, 7.30 pm*
Written, directed by and starring Julie Delpy, this is an intelligent romantic comedy about a French photographer and her American boyfriend on a two-day visit to her family in Paris. It also stars Delpy's real-life parents and her cat, Max.

YEELEN *Mali, 105 min, Fri 3 Nov, 8.00 pm*
The classic 1987 drama by Malian film-maker Souleymane Cissé. Yeelen is set in the 13th century and tells the story of Niankoro, a young man who uses magic to fight his father, a dangerous magician.

⁞ FAMILY FILM ⁞
RATATOUILLE *USA, 111 min, Saturday 4 Nov, 11.30 am, 3.00 pm & 6.30 pm*
Rémy, a rat, wants to be a chef. He comes to Paris and makes friends with Alfredo Linguini, a young man who works in the kitchen of a famous restaurant. Animated fun for all the family.

Box Office The Picture House, Hay Street, Perth   **Ticket Prices** Adults $13.50. Over 60s / students / under 15s $9.00

3 **Read the programme again. What films can you see if you:**

1 like serious films?
2 want to have a good laugh?
3 are busy in the evening?
4 want to take your children to the cinema?
5 enjoy long films?

Choosing a film

Jon and Mia from Perth, Australia

VOCABULARY

Suggestions

1 a Jon and Mia decide to go to the cinema. Complete their conversation.

| Why don't we ...   Would you like to ...   OK.   We could ...   I don't know. |

MIA   Some of these films look quite interesting.
JON   Yeah, that's true. _____ go and see one some time this week?
MIA   Yeah, _____ . _____ see *Family Law*? I heard it's really good.
JON   Hm, _____ . It sounds a bit boring. _____ see *The Others*.
MIA   Well, I don't usually like horror films, but that one sounds good.

b 🔊 **3.2 Listen to check.**

2 a Put the expressions from 1a in the correct groups.

Making suggestions *Why don't we ...*	Saying yes	Saying no / not sure

b Add these expressions to the correct groups in 2a.

| Good idea.   Fine with me.   I don't really want to.   Let's ...
That sounds good.   I'm not sure.   No, thanks. |

3 Practise the conversation in 1a with different expressions. Take turns to be Jon and Mia.

SPEAKING

4 a You're going to The Picture House with a group of friends. Choose two films from the programme you'd like to see, and two films you don't want to see.

b In groups, decide which film to see together.

5 In pairs, ask and answer the questions.

1 How often do you watch films at the cinema?
2 When was the last time you saw a film? What was it? Did you enjoy it?
3 Do you ever watch films more than once? Give examples.
4 Do you like watching films from other countries? Give examples.

What are you doing tonight?

10.2 goals
⊚ make and respond to suggestions
⊚ make arrangements to meet

READING

1 **a** Look at the picture and read the first email. Can you guess how Kimiko answers Jon's questions?

Kimiko from Perth

File Edit View Insert Format Tools Message Help

Hi Kimiko,
How's your day going? And what are you doing tonight? I'm going to the cinema with Mia. Want to come with us?
Jon.

Delete Reply Reply All Forward Print

Hello Jon,
Not a good day at the office – I'm having lots of problems. Yes, let's go out tonight. Text me – I'm in a meeting this afternoon.
K.

b Read Kimiko's reply. Check your ideas.

2 Read the texts Jon and Kimiko send later. Put them in order from 1–6.

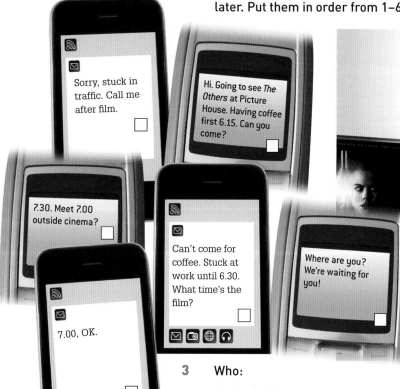

Sorry, stuck in traffic. Call me after film.

Hi. Going to see *The Others* at Picture House. Having coffee first 6.15. Can you come?

7.30. Meet 7.00 outside cinema?

Can't come for coffee. Stuck at work until 6.30. What time's the film?

Where are you? We're waiting for you!

7.00, OK.

Jon and Mia

3 Who:

1 invited Kimiko to the cinema?
2 had coffee together?
3 had a difficult day?
4 saw the film?
5 couldn't get to the cinema on time?

LISTENING

4 🎧 **3.3** Listen to Jon and Kimiko's phone call after the film. Can they meet this week?

5 🎧 **3.3** Listen again.

1 Where are Jon and Mia going now?
2 Does Kimiko want to go with them? Why? / Why not?
3 What are Kimiko's plans for Friday? What are her plans for Monday?

Arrangements

GRAMMAR

Present progressive for future arrangements

Meet Kimiko at airport MONDAY 11PM

Tues.
shopping: chicken, mushrooms, cream, fruit.
8.00 – cook dinner for Mia.

Meet Mia Thursday lunchtime, 1pm. Get present for Gillian.

Silver Court Dental Practice

Name: Jon Ellis
Date & time: Thursday 9th Nov., 4pm
Dentist: Dr Vernon

Friday: Gillian's birthday party, Royston cafe (from 6pm)

Grammar reference and practice, R-8

1 Look at sentences 1–8 in the table and answer the questions.

a   Which **two** sentences are about now?

b   Which **six** sentences are about future arrangements?

> ❓
> ¹What **are you doing** tonight?
>
> ➕
> ²I'm **going** to the cinema with Mia.
> ³We're **having** coffee first at 6.15. Can you come?
> ⁴Where are you? We're **waiting** for you!
> ⁵We're **walking** to Delmonico's now for a pizza.
> ⁶I'm **flying** to Singapore this Friday.
> ⁷I'm **coming** back on Monday night.
>
> ➖
> ⁸You're **not going** for work, I hope.

2 Look at the underlined future time expressions in the table. Add these expressions to the correct groups. Some can go in more than one group.

> 12 March   year   tomorrow   11 o'clock   December   evening

- tonight	at 6.15	on Monday night	this Friday	next	in

3 **a** Work in A/B pairs. A, look at Jon's arrangements for next week on the left. B, look at Kimiko's diary on R-1.

b Tell each other about Jon's and Kimiko's arrangements. How many times will Jon and Kimiko see each other next week?

> Jon's meeting Kimiko at the airport on Monday at 11 pm.

PRONUNCIATION

Compound nouns

4 **a** 🔊 **3.4** Listen to these compound nouns (nouns made from two different nouns). Notice that the stress is on the *first* word. ❶ Practise saying the words.

a ●phone call   a ●sales meeting   ●football practice   a ●birthday party

b Underline the stress in these compound nouns.

a c•offee break   a yoga class   a guitar lesson   a tennis match   a cinema programme

c 🔊 **3.5** Listen to check. ❶ Practise saying the compound nouns.

SPEAKING

What are you doing tomorrow lunchtime?

I think I'm free.

I'm not, sorry. I'm going to the shops.

5 **a** You want to go for a coffee with friends. Write down four times when you're free.

1   tomorrow, 11am
2   Monday, 8pm
3   Tuesday, 2pm
4   Friday evening

b In groups, arrange a time to meet.

c When are you meeting? Tell the class.

Arrange a film night

10.3 goals

◎ talk about films
◎ make and respond to suggestions
◎ make arrangements to meet

Reeta   Jane   Matthew

TASK LISTENING

1 How often do you watch films at home? When? Who with?

2 🎧 **3.6** Listen to Jane, Reeta and Matthew arranging a film night at Reeta's home.

1 When are they going to meet?
2 Tick (✔) the films they talk about.
Pan's Labyrinth ☐   Casablanca ☐   The Bourne Supremacy ☐   Yeelen ☐
3 Which film do they decide to watch?

TASK VOCABULARY

Talking about films

3 a Match 1–4 with a–d.

1 What's it like?
2 Who's in it?
3 What's it about?
4 It's about this young man with magical powers.

a It's about a young girl and it's set in Spain ... in the 1940s, I think.
b That sounds interesting.
c Matt Damon.
d Well, it's an action film, I guess.

b Read the script on R-15 to check.

c In pairs, test each other. Take turns to say 1–4 and remember a–d.

TASK

4 a You want to watch a film at home with some friends. Think about:

• when you're free this week.
• two films you'd like to see.
• how to describe the films.

b Talk in groups. Decide:

• when to meet.
• where to meet.
• which film to watch.

c Tell other groups what you decided.

Keyword *about*

1 Which sentences use about with a topic? Which use it with a number? <u>Underline</u> the topics and numbers.

> 1 *Family Law* is about the difficult relationship between a father and son. Unit 10
> 2 I've got an idea. I read about this film called *Yeelen*. Unit 10
> 3 I first met Ed when he was about sixteen. Unit 8
> 4 So, Min, what do you think about <u>New Year</u>? Unit 3

about with topics

2 a Match 1–7 with a–g to make conversations.

1 "You look stressed. Is there a problem?"	a "Hmm. I don't know. I'll think about it."
2 "Can I see the room this evening?"	b "Yes, there is! Do you know anything about computers?"
3 "Do you know that Dave's getting married?"	c "Sure. How about six thirty?"
4 "Don't forget the party on Friday."	d "It was terrible! I don't want to talk about it."
5 "Hello, can I help you?"	e "What party? No one told me about that."
6 "How was your day?"	f "Yes, please. I have a question about my ticket."
7 "So, do you want to buy these jeans?"	g "Yes, I heard about that."

b 🔊 **3.7** Listen to check. Practise the conversations.

c Test each other in pairs. Take turns to say 1–7 and remember a–g.

about with numbers

3 a Talk in teams. Guess the answers. Use about.

1 When did Yuri Gagarin go into space?
2 How many teeth does an adult elephant have?
3 When were the first modern Olympics?
4 How high is Mount Everest?
5 How many people are there in a cricket team?
6 How long is the Great Wall of China?
7 How long does it take for light to travel from the sun to the earth?
8 When did people start writing?

Gagarin went into space in about 1960, I think.

Was it 1962?

b 🔊 **3.8** Listen to check. Which team has the best guesses?

Independent learning Reading the phonemic script 2: vowels

1 a You can use the *Sounds of English* chart on R-20 to help you with the pronunciation of new words, for example when you find them in a dictionary. Match symbols 1–12 with the sounds in these words.

¹æ	²ɑː	³e	⁴ɜː	⁵ɪ	⁶iː	⁷ɒ	⁸ɔː	⁹ʌ	¹⁰ʊ	¹¹uː	¹²ə

> **documentary** /ˌdɒkjəˈmentᵊri/ *noun*
> (*plural* **documentaries**)
> a film or television programme that gives facts about a real situation
>
> *Cambridge Essential English Dictionary*

black [1] but ☐ first ☐ lot ☐ good ☐ help ☐
park ☐ food ☐ sister ☐ six ☐ meet ☐ sport ☐

b 🔊 **3.9** Listen to check.

2 a Can you read these words from units 8–10? How do we say them?

1 /ˈhɒrə/
2 /ˈmɔːnɪŋ/
3 /ˈkɒmədiː/
4 /ˈbjuːtɪfəl/
5 /ˈmʌðə/
6 /məˈstɑːʃ/

b 🔊 **3.10** Listen to check.

3 a Match the words with the same vowel sound.

b Use a dictionary to check your answers, or look at the key on R-3.

boot car floor
fruit full good got
learn love met niece
short speak start sun
wash went worse

Goals
- write and reply to an invitation
- write a thank-you note

1 In pairs, ask and answer the questions.

1 When was the last time you got together with old friends? What did you do?
2 How do you usually invite people to your home: by email, phone, text, or face to face?

2 a Put emails A–C in order.

A ☐

Thank you so much for Saturday. We had a fantastic time and it was great to see Paul and the kids again. You organised everything so well – I hope you had a good time too! I must invite you and Paul to dinner soon.

Love, Ana.

B ☐

This is to invite you (and your families) to my 30th birthday party on December 15th. I'd like to book Toni's restaurant for the afternoon and evening (have a look at their website). Please let me know if you can come (and how many) so I can book it as soon as possible. I'll ask you again nearer the time. I hope you can come.

Claudia. X

C ☐

Sounds absolutely fantastic, Claudia. Toni's looks lovely. We'd love to come.

Ana.

b Put text messages D–H in order.

D ☐

Friday's good. See you then.
C

E ☐

Lovely evening. Thanks Ana. Let's get together again soon.
Cx

F ☐

Can you and Paul come to dinner this Saturday (17th)? About 8?
Ana

G ☐

Going away (rock climbing!), but free on Friday evening, 23rd. OK?
Ana

H ☐

Sorry, Paul's away this weekend. Are you free next weekend?
Claudia

3 Read all the emails and text messages again. Which are invitations? replies? thank-you notes?

4 a Cover the emails and text messages. Match the beginnings and endings of the invitations.

1 This is to invite you to
2 I'd like to
3 Please let me know
4 I hope you
5 Are you free
6 Can you and Jon come to dinner

a if you can come.
b next weekend?
c this Saturday?
d book Toni's restaurant.
e my 30th birthday party.
f can come.

b Look at the invitations to check. Can you think of more ways to complete 1–6?

This is to invite you to my flat for dinner.

5 Complete these expressions from the replies and thank-you notes.

1 We had a …
2 It was great …
3 Sounds …
4 We'd love …
5 Friday's …
6 Lovely …
7 Let's get together …
8 Sorry, …

6 *Ellipsis* In emails and texts, we often don't use words like *I, we, be, do, that, the*, etc.

~~That was a~~ Lovely evening.
~~We're~~ Going away (rock climbing!) but ~~we're~~ free on Friday evening.

Make these sentences shorter for an email or text. Cross out the words you don't need.

1 That sounds absolutely fantastic.
2 I'm very busy this weekend. I can't come to the picnic. I hope you have a good time.
3 It was lovely to see you. Do you want to meet again next weekend?
4 We're going to see *The Others* at the Picture House. We're having coffee first.

7 a Choose an event and write an email invitation.

- a birthday party   • a graduation party   • a picnic   • something else

b Read another student's invitation. Write a reply.

c Imagine it's after the event. Write a short note to say thank you.

Review

VOCABULARY Suggestions

1 a 🔊 **3.11** Listen to Suzi and Michelle. What do they want to do?

b 🔊 **3.11** Listen two more times. Write down as many words as you can.

SUZI	So Michelle, _____ _____ _____ _____ _____ _____ tomorrow?
MICHELLE	Hm, not really. _____ _____ _____ _____ _____ Heidelberg?
SUZI	That _____ _____ . _____ _____ _____ some shopping.
MICHELLE	Hm, _____ _____ _____ . _____ _____ the castle.
SUZI	All right. _____ _____ _____ _____ _____ a coat.

c Work together to complete the conversation. Then read the script on R-16 to check.

d Find expressions in the conversations for:

- making suggestions
- saying yes   • saying no

e You're going to plan a day trip to another town or city. Think about:

- where to go   • what to do
- how to get there   • when to go

f Plan your trip in groups. Then tell the class what you decided.

GRAMMAR Present progressive for arrangements

2 a What questions can you ask about this sentence?

I'm going to Brno this weekend.
Why ...? Who ...? Where ...? How long ...? How ...?

b Take a piece of paper and:

1 Write four of your arrangements for this month. Exchange papers with a partner.
2 Write one or two questions about each of your partner's sentences. Give back the paper.
3 Write answers to the questions.

c Put away the paper and tell a group about your partner's arrangements. Can you remember all the information correctly?

CAN YOU REMEMBER? Unit 9 – Getting information

3 a Put the words in order to make questions.

1 here / Are / there / any bookshops / near ?
2 get there / to / What's / way / the best ?
3 long / it / take / does / How ?
4 What / it / open / does / time ?

b Ask and answer the questions.

c Change the word *bookshops* in 1 and have two more conversations.

Extension

SPELLING AND SOUNDS g

4 a 🔊 **3.12** We can say g in two ways. Read and listen to the words in the table.

/g/	/dʒ/ g + e, i, y
go again big good great grammar	arrangements page magic religion gym Egypt

b Add these words to the correct group.

agree colleague college dangerous engineer green group message technology

c Some common words don't follow the rule. Practise saying them.

begin get forget girl give together

d 🔊 **3.13** Spellcheck. Close your book. Listen and write twelve words. Check your spelling on R-16.

NOTICE sounds + adjective

5 a Find the conversations from this unit (on R-16) and complete the expressions with sounds.

1	MIA	Would you like to see *Family Law*?
	JON	It sounds a bit _____ .
2	JON	We could see *The Others*.
	MIA	Well, I don't usually like horror films, but that one sounds _____ .
3	REETA	Would you like to come over to my place and watch a film?
	JANE	Yeah, that sounds _____ , Reeta.
4	JANE	It's about this young man with magical powers.
	MATTHEW	That sounds _____ .

b Which expressions are positive? Which are negative? Think of more adjectives you can use.

c In groups, make a list of films which are on at the cinema at the moment, or are coming soon.

1 Tell each other what you know about the films.
2 Guess what the films are like. Use sounds.

Self-assessment

Can you do these things in English? Circle a number on each line. 1 = I can't do this, 5 = I can do this well.

talk about films	1	2	3	4	5
find information in a cinema programme	1	2	3	4	5
make and respond to suggestions	1	2	3	4	5
make arrangements to meet	1	2	3	4	5
write and reply to an invitation	1	2	3	4	5
write a thank-you note	1	2	3	4	5

- For Wordcards, reference and saving your work → e-Portfolio
- For more practice → Self-study Pack, Unit 10

Journeys

At the airport

1 Do you ever travel by plane? Do you like flying? Why? / Why not?

A

B
Heathrow
Boarding gate B38
B38

C
Welcome to Japan

D
⚠WARNING
X RAY

E

F
←出口
Exit

2 a Match these places with pictures A–F.

> boarding gate   check-in   security
> baggage collection   customs   passport control

OK, you go to the check-in, then ...

b What parts of the airport do you have to go through before you fly? What about when you arrive? Put the places in order.

CHECK IN
⇐

Belinda from Spain

3 a Look at Belinda's boarding pass.

1 Where's she travelling to?
2 What airline is she using?
3 What time's her flight?

b Find Belinda's flight on the board.

1 Is her flight on time?
2 What time's it leaving?
3 What gate's it leaving from?

BRITISH AIRWAYS ➤ **BOARDING PASS**   BRITISH AIRWAYS ➤

GATE	GATE OPENS	SEAT
20	11:55	23K

RAMOS/BELINDA MISS (ADT)
BA 0059   27 AUG   12:35   LONDON LHR
TOKYO NRT

NAME
RAMOS/BELINDA MISS
FROM LONDON   LHR
TO   TOKYO   NRT

FLIGHT	DATE	TIME
BA 0059	27 AUG	12:35

GATE	SEAT
20	23K

Destination			Departure			
Code	City	Flight	Scheduled	Actual	Gate	Status
DUB	Dublin	EI 153	11:50 AM	-	-	Cancelled
FCO	Rome	BA 548	12:20 PM	12:20 PM	4	Boarding
BOM	Mumbai	AI 119	12:20 PM	12:40 PM	11	Delayed
KUL	Kuala Lumpur	MH 329	12:25 PM	12:25 PM	21	On time
NRT	Tokyo	BA 0059	12:35 PM	12:45 PM	20	Delayed
YYC	Calgary	AC 851	12:45 PM	12:45 PM	18	On time

Getting a flight

LISTENING

1 a **3.14** Listen to Belinda checking in. What does she give the person?

b **3.14** Listen again. Complete 1–5.

1 Can I see your _____ , please?
2 Do you have any _____ luggage?
3 Did you pack your _____ yourself?
4 Are you carrying _____ for anyone else?
5 Boarding is at _____ from _____ 20.

c Match 1–5 with Belinda's answers a–e.

a Here you are. b Thanks. c Just this bag. d Yes, I did. e No.

d **3.15** Listen to the sentences in b and give answers.

2 a **3.16** Listen to Belinda. Where is she now?

b **3.16** Listen again. Tick (✓) every time you hear these things.

bag belt keys laptop shoes wallet mobile

c Complete the conversation with words from 2b. Write them in the gaps on the right.

OFFICER 1	1?	1 _____
BELINDA	I've put them in my 2.	2 _____
OFFICER 1	OK. Is there a 3 in here?	3 _____
BELINDA	No.	
OFFICER 1	And your 4, please.	4 _____
BELINDA	Oh, OK.	
OFFICER 2	Come forward, please. 5? 6?	5 _____ 6 _____
BELINDA	Uh, they're in my 7.	7 _____
OFFICER 2	8?	8 _____
BELINDA	That too.	
OFFICER 2	Are you wearing a 9?	9 _____
BELINDA	Oh yes, sorry.	
OFFICER 2	That's fine, thank you.	
BELINDA	Thanks.	
OFFICER 3	Could you open your 10, please?	10 _____
BELINDA	OK.	
OFFICER 3	That's fine. Enjoy your trip.	
BELINDA	Thanks.	

d **3.16** Listen again to check.

PRONUNCIATION
Polite intonation

3 a **3.17** Listen to each of these expressions, said twice. Which one sounds more polite, A or B? Why?

1 Oh yes, sorry. A / B
2 That's fine, thank you. A / B
3 Thanks. A / B
4 That's fine. Enjoy your trip. A / B

b Practise saying the expressions politely. **P**

4 a In pairs, practise Belinda's conversation at security.

b Cover the words 1–10 and practise again.

SPEAKING

5 a Work in groups of three. You're at an airport. Look at your role cards and complete them.

A, you work at **check-in**. Look on R-1.
B, you work for **airport security**. Look on R-4.
C, you're a **passenger**. Look on R-5.

b Have two conversations: one at check-in, and the other at security.

6 Change roles and have the conversations again.

A traveller's tale

READING

1 a Match the pictures and the words.

a bear   a snake   a pigeon   a spider   a rat   a bat

Ⓐ    Ⓑ    Ⓒ    Ⓓ 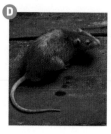   Ⓔ    Ⓕ

b Do you have these animals in your country? How do you feel about them?

2 Read the story. What was Belinda frightened of? What was the receptionist frightened of?

TRAVELLERS' TALES

Help!

Belinda Ramos works for a large IT company and travels whenever she can. She's visited Belgium, Lebanon, England, France, Germany, Japan and Mexico. She'd love to go to Africa one day.

I was in the south of Japan at the time. One morning, I woke up in my hotel room, opened my eyes and looked around my room. The first thing I saw was a huge spider on the wall. It was about ten centimetres across. I hate spiders! I ran out of the room to the reception desk and shouted for help. "Kuma!" I remembered from my Japanese lessons that 'kuma' means 'spider'.
"Kuma?" the receptionist said.
"Kuma!" I shouted again. "In my room!"

"Kuma?"
"KUMA!!!"
The receptionist looked really frightened. She picked up the phone and said something quickly in Japanese. About a minute later – and I'm not joking – a policeman with a gun ran into the hotel and went into my room. For a minute there was silence but then we heard a laugh, so we went in. When the receptionist saw the spider on the wall, she started laughing too.
In Japanese, spider is 'kumo'. 'Kuma' means 'bear'.

3 Read the story again. Who:

1   took Japanese lessons?
2   shouted 'Kuma'?
3   made a phone call?
4   looked frightened?
5   went into Belinda's room first?
6   laughed?

4 What words in your language do learners sometimes mix up?

GRAMMAR
Articles

5 Look at the examples from Belinda's story and ⟨circle⟩ the correct form in the grammar box.

Use *a / the /* no article when you talk about a person or thing for the first time:
The first thing I saw was **a** huge spider on the wall.

Use *a / the /* no article when the reader or listener knows *which* thing:
When the receptionist saw **the spider** on the wall, she started laughing too.

Use *a / the /* no article when you talk about things in general.
I hate spiders!

6 You use the in a lot of fixed expressions and before some adjectives. Add expressions 1–3 from Belinda's story to the table on p93.

I was ¹in the south of Japan ²at the time.
³The first thing I saw was a huge spider on the wall.

Time expressions	Place expressions	Before some adjectives
in the morning	in the middle of ...	the best, the worst, the most
at the weekend	in the corner of ...	the same
at the moment	at the end of ...	the last, the next

7 **a** Complete the sentences with **a**, **an**, **the**, or no article.

1 When was *the* last time you saw a spider?
2 Do you like _____ pasta?
3 Is there _____ art gallery near here?
4 Can you open _____ door, please?
5 Have you got _____ pen I can use?
6 What's _____ name of the person next to you?
7 Do you like _____ cats?
8 What's _____ easiest language to learn?

b 🔊 **3.18** Listen to check. How do you usually say **a**, **an** and **the**? How do you say **the** in sentence 8? Why? **P**

Grammar reference and practice, R-9

c Write two or three more questions with expressions from the table in 6.

d Ask and answer all the questions.

Telling a story

VOCABULARY

Storytelling expressions

1 **a** Which expressions in the box:

1 start a story? 2 link a story? 3 end a story?

> Later, ...   It was two in the morning.   It was really strange.
> ... and then ...   I was with some friends.   In the end, ...   After that, ...
> I had a great time.   Well, this was a few weeks ago.

b 🔊 **3.19** Listen to check. **P**

SPEAKING

2 **a** Work in A/B pairs. A, look at these pictures and read Holly's story here. B, look at the pictures and read Jack's story on R-4.

> in my car in the Rocky Mountains in Canada ➜ lots of mountains and trees ➜ see a family of bears, mother and two cubs ➜ stop car ➜ get out and take photos ➜ cubs look frightened, mother gets angry ➜ walks towards me ➜ can't open car door ...

b Think of a good ending for Holly's story. Imagine you are Holly. Prepare to tell the story. Think about:

- the past simple of the verbs (see > saw).
- where to use **the** (stop **the** car; **the** mother bear).
- where to use storytelling expressions. (Later, ...)

> Well, this was a couple of years ago. I was in my car in the Rocky Mountains ...

3 Work in A/B pairs. Tell your stories.

4 🔊 **3.20** Now listen to both stories. Are the endings like yours?

Describe a journey

11.3 goals
- tell a story
- talk about a journey

TASK LISTENING

1 **a** Look at the pictures of Sam's journey. What do you think happened?

b ⏵ **3.21** Listen to the story of Sam's journey. Were you right?

TASK VOCABULARY

Talking about a journey

2 **a** Circle the correct words in the sentences about Sam's journey.

1. He drove to / flew to the airport.
2. The flight was delayed / cancelled.
3. He booked a seat on another flight / a room in a hotel.
4. He spent two hours / all night at the airport.
5. The airport was comfortable / uncomfortable.
6. He caught / missed the plane to Dublin.
7. The plane took off / landed at nine o'clock.
8. It had to go to Cork, in the north / in the south of Ireland.
9. He stayed in a five-star hotel / a youth hostel.
10. He had a great time / a terrible time there.

b ⏵ **3.22** Listen to check. **P**

TASK

3 **a** Think of two or three of your own journeys. For example, a time when:

- you missed a flight or a train.
- something interesting happened.
- you saw something interesting.
- you had a very long journey.

b Prepare to tell your stories. Think about the questions.

1. When was it?
2. What was the reason for your journey?
3. What happened?
4. How did you feel?

4 Tell each other about your journeys. Which journeys were fun? Which were difficult?

Keyword *at*

1 Add the highlighted expressions to the table.

> 1 I was in the south of Japan at the time. Unit 11
> 2 Middle children are good at meeting new people. Unit 8
> 3 I met Ed when he was about 16. I was at his father's house. Unit 8
> 4 I watch the fireworks at midnight from the window. Unit 3
> 5 We were best friends at school. Unit 1
> 6 She wasn't at the party. Unit 1

times	places	group events	*good at ...*
at 7.00 at the moment	at home at work at John's flat	at a lecture at a match	good at English not very good at driving

2 a Add at to sentences 1–8.

Find someone who ...

1 was a party last night.
2 met their husband or wife school.
3 works home a lot.
4 is reading a good book the moment.
5 often works the weekend.
6 was a wedding recently.
7 is good sport.
8 isn't very good geography.

Were you at a party last night?

Yes, I was.

Where was it?

b Use the sentences in 2a to ask questions to other students.
Try to find out more information.

Across cultures Saying sorry

1 The word sorry has a lot of different uses in English. Match pictures A–E with situations 1–5.

A Sorry, but there's a problem with my shower.

B Sorry, is this the train to Bristol?

C Oh, I'm sorry!

D Sorry?

E I'm very sorry, your card's not working.

You can use sorry when:
1 you want to apologise.
2 you don't understand or can't hear someone.
3 you ask for information from people you don't know.
4 you want to complain about something.
5 you give bad news.

2 Read what people from different countries say about saying sorry, and discuss the questions in pairs.

" In Spain you use different words to say *sorry*. When you can't hear something you say *perdón?* or *qué?* When you want to complain you say *lo lamento* or *discúlpame* or *lo siento*. MANUEL "

" In Britain, people apologise a lot. When you bump into someone, or when someone bumps into you, both people usually say *sorry*. MATTHEW "

" In Sudan if you are not happy about something you just complain about it, you don't say *sorry*. KHALID "

" In Switzerland the word for sorry is *Entschuldigung* but if we can't hear someone we don't normally say *sorry*, we just say *what? uh?* NATHALIE "

1 Does your language have one word for saying sorry, or different words for different situations?
2 Do you think people apologise a lot in your country? What about other countries you know?
3 What do you say in situations 1–5?

Ben

Nina

Goals
◉ ask questions to develop a conversation
◉ change the topic of a conversation

NINA	Hi, Ben. ¹How are you?
BEN	Fine thanks. Are you okay?
NINA	Yes, not bad. ²Did you see *The Family* on TV last night?
BEN	Yeah.
NINA	³What happened? I missed it.
BEN	Erm, Dario left his job and Jon asked Anna to marry him. It was, er, pretty boring actually.
NINA	Jon asked Anna to marry him? Really? ⁴What did she say?
BEN	Erm, I don't know.
NINA	What do you mean you don't know? Did she say yes?
BEN	Well, actually, I stopped watching before the end. ⁵Anyway, ⁶what did you do last night?
NINA	Oh, we went out for a meal. It was really nice. But I forgot my credit card and we didn't have any cash.
BEN	Oh no, ⁷what did you do?
NINA	I had to drive home and get the credit card while Sam and the kids had dessert.
BEN	Oh, that's too bad.
NINA	Yeah.
BEN	⁸So, ⁹how's your family?
NINA	Oh, fine. Adriana starts school next week …

1 Look at the picture. Where do Nina and Ben work?

2 🔊 3.23 Listen to their conversation. Tick (✓) the things they talk about.

a TV programme ✓   friends   the cinema
last night   a meal   a concert   a wedding

3 Read the script. Complete the notes with the highlighted expressions from the script.

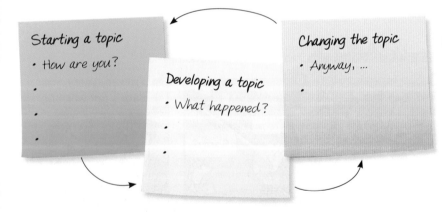

Starting a topic
• How are you?
•
•
•

Developing a topic
• What happened?
•
•

Changing the topic
• Anyway, …
•

4 a Complete this conversation with expressions from 3, and your own ideas.

A Hi. How are you?
B Good, thanks. Are you okay?
A Yes, fine thanks. _____?
B No, I was too tired.
A _____?
B Just watched TV.
A Oh, _____?
B Yes, I always watch it but I missed the ending. _____?
A Well, the wedding didn't happen in the end.
B Oh, you're joking.
A No, and that was the last show. _____, what have we got to do today?
B Well, we need to check all these …

b In pairs, practise the conversation. Take turns to start.

5 a It's Monday morning. You're going to have a conversation with your colleague.
  • Think about the questions you can ask to start the conversation.
  • Think about your answers to the questions.

b Start the conversation. Try to keep your conversation going for one or two minutes.

6 How long were your conversations? What was the most popular topic?

11 Look again ♻

Review

VOCABULARY Airports

1 a Complete the words with vowels.

1 b__rd_ng g_te
2 ch_ck-_n
3 s_c_r_ty
4 b_gg_ge c_ll_ct__n
5 c_st_ms
6 p_ssp_rt c_ntr_l

b Where can you hear these sentences?

1 Do you have any hand luggage?
2 Are you wearing a belt?
3 Could you open your bag, please?
4 Are you carrying anything for anyone else?
5 Come forward, please.
6 Boarding is at 12.15 from gate 20.
7 Did you pack your bag yourself?
8 Can I see your boarding pass, please?

c Ask and answer the questions in b.

GRAMMAR Articles

2 a Complete the questions with a, an, the, or no article.

1 How many _____ international airports are there in your country? Where are they?
2 What's _____ biggest one? How many terminals does it have?
3 Do you have _____ central train station in your city? What's the name of _____ station?
4 Do people use _____ buses to travel around your city? What about your country? How comfortable are they?
5 Does your city have _____ underground? How many lines does _____ underground have?
6 What other _____ kinds of transport do people use where you live?

b Ask and answer the questions.

CAN YOU REMEMBER? Unit 10 – Suggestions

3 a Look at the suggestion. Think of other expressions to replace Why don't we ...?

Why don't we go out for a meal?

b Think of suggestions for a person in these situations.

1 I want to drive to the airport but my car is at the garage.
2 I'm bored. I have no money to go out.
3 My neighbour is playing very loud music.
4 I'm in an English lesson and I feel ill.
5 It's 4 o'clock in the morning and I can't sleep.
6 I'm hungry, but I don't have any food at home to cook.

c Compare your suggestions. Say what you think about each other's ideas.

Extension

SPELLING AND SOUNDS ng

4 a ▶ 3.24 You can say -ng in two ways. Listen and practise saying the words.

/ŋ/	/ŋg/
flying	England

b Add these words to the correct groups. What's the rule?

skiing   long   longer   running
thing   stronger   youngest

c ▶ 3.25 Listen to check. Practise saying the words.

d ▶ 3.26 Spellcheck. Close your books. Listen to six words and write them down.

e Check your spelling.

NOTICE start and stop

5 a After start and stop, you can often use a verb + -ing:

When the receptionist saw the spider on the wall, she started laughing.
Well, actually, I stopped watching before the end.

Complete sentences 1–5 with these words:

running   shouting   boarding
eating   playing

1 Can you ask your children to stop _____ around the airport lounge?
2 Passengers with children can start _____ now.
3 Please start _____ before your meal gets cold.
4 Could you stop _____ and talk more quietly?
5 I started _____ the guitar when I was about eight years old.

b Talk about your present and past interests or habits.

1 When did you start doing them? Did you stop? When? Why?
2 Is there anything you would like to start doing, or stop doing?

Self-assessment

Can you do these things in English? Circle a number on each line. 1 = I can't do this, 5 = I can do this well.

◎ check in and board a flight	1	2	3	4	5
◎ tell a story	1	2	3	4	5
◎ talk about a journey	1	2	3	4	5
◎ ask questions to develop a conversation	1	2	3	4	5
◎ change the topic of a conversation	1	2	3	4	5

• For Wordcards, reference and saving your work → e-Portfolio
• For more practice → Self-study Pack, Unit 11

12

12.1 goals
- talk about health
- buy things in a pharmacy
- understand instructions on medicines

Are you OK?

I've got a headache

1 a Do the quiz. Circle your answers.

BODY SENSE: *Test your knowledge*

1 Your head weighs about 3.5 / 5.5 / 8.5 kilos.
2 The stomach can hold four / six / eight litres of food.
3 You use 5 / 12 / 20 muscles to smile. You use about 50 / 70 / 80 muscles to speak.
4 Our eyes never grow / stop growing. Our nose and ears never grow / stop growing.
5 The body loses half a kilo / more than half a kilo / a kilo of skin every year.
6 Over 20% / 40% / 50% of the bones in your body are in your hands and feet.
7 The smallest bone is in your ear / nose / little toe. It's the size of a grain of rice.
8 Your thumb is the same length as your nose / big toe / ear.
9 Children have 18 / 20 / 22 first teeth. Adults have 28 / 30 / 32 teeth.
10 Your heart beats about 50,000 / 100,000 / 200,000 times every day.

b 🔊 3.27 Listen to check.

2 Look at the highlighted words in the quiz. What other body words do you know? Check in Vocabulary reference, *The body*, R-13.

3 a Match problems 1-8 with pictures A–H.

I've got a	¹headache. ²cold . ³sore throat. ⁴temperature.
	⁵pain in my back. ⁶problem with my knee.
I feel (really / a bit)	⁷sick. ⁸tired.

A  B C  D  E  F  G  H

b 🔊 3.28 Listen to check. **P**

4 Make conversations. Talk about different problems from 3a.

| Are you OK? / Are you all right? | ⟹ | Yes, I'm OK, thanks.
Yes, I'm fine. |

⟱

| Not really. / No, not too good.
I've got a ...
I feel ... | ⟹ | Oh, I'm sorry about that.
I'm sorry to hear that. |

What are your symptoms?

Marc, from Lyons in
France, is in the UK on
a work trip. He goes to
a pharmacy.

1 🔊 **3.29** Listen to the first part of Marc's conversation with the pharmacist.
What problems does Marc have?

2 Match the pharmacist's questions with Marc's answers.

1 What are your symptoms?
2 Are you allergic to anything?
3 Are you taking any other medicine?

a Just dairy products.
b No, not at the moment.
c I've got a pain in my back.

3 a Read the medicine packages below. Which medicine is best for Marc? Why?

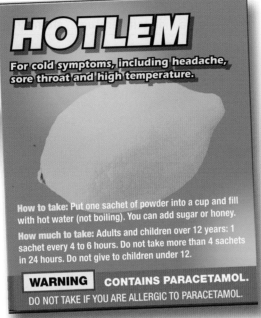

HOTLEM

**For cold symptoms, including headache,
sore throat and high temperature.**

How to take: Put one sachet of powder into a cup and fill
with hot water (not boiling). You can add sugar or honey.

How much to take: Adults and children over 12 years: 1
sachet every 4 to 6 hours. Do not take more than 4 sachets
in 24 hours. Do not give to children under 12.

WARNING CONTAINS PARACETAMOL.

DO NOT TAKE IF YOU ARE ALLERGIC TO PARACETAMOL.

Paracetamol

500 mg tablets

**For the relief of aches
and pains, including
headache and toothache.**

KEEP AWAY FROM CHILDREN

Do not take with alcohol.
If symptoms continue, go to your doctor.

DOSE: Adults and children over 12 years:
1 to 2 tablets every 4 to 6 hours. Do not take
more than 8 tablets in 24 hours. Children 6
to 12 years: half to one tablet every 4 to 6
hours. Do not take more than 4 tablets in
24 hours. Not for children under 6.

b 🔊 **3.30** Listen to the second part of Marc's conversation.
Does he buy Hotlem or paracetamol?

4 Read the packages again. Are these sentences true or false?

1 You shouldn't give Hotlem to a ten year-old.
2 Hotlem has paracetamol in it.
3 An adult can take six sachets of Hotlem in 24 hours.
4 You can drink wine with paracetamol.
5 An adult shouldn't have more than eight tablets in 24 hours.
6 You can give paracetamol to a five year-old.

5 a 🔊 **3.31** Listen to sentences from Marc's conversation. Notice how a consonant at the
end of a word links to a vowel at the beginning of the next word.

1 Do you need‿any help?
2 What‿are your symptoms?
3 I've had the headache for‿about‿an hour.
4 I've got‿a pain‿in my back.
5 This‿is the best thing.

Do you need‿any help?
consonant   vowel

b Practise saying the sentences.

6 a Work in A/B pairs. A, you're the pharmacist.
B, you feel ill. Have a conversation and buy
some medicine.

Hello. Can I help you?

Yes. I'd like something for ...

b Change roles and have another conversation.

Home remedies

READING

1 What do you do in situations 1–4? Do you:

- take a day off work?
- ask someone for advice?
- see a doctor or dentist?
- go to a pharmacy?
- take some medicine?
- do nothing?
- do something else?

1 You've got toothache.
2 You feel tired and you have no energy.
3 You've got a temperature.
4 You've got a really bad pain in your back and you don't know why.

> Maybe onions can help stomach ache.

2 a Pictures A–D show different remedies. Can you match them with these problems?

> headache   toothache   a high temperature   stomach ache

A

black toast with honey

B
an onion

C

a wet teabag

D

salt water

b Read the web postings to check your ideas.

---

http://www.knowledge.com/homeremedies

KNOWLEDGE.COM

The world's best advice site ... written by you.

Home Remedies

Monica, Canada
April 24 10.41

Black toast with honey
A friend of mine stayed in a hotel in India and the manager gave this to her for stomach ache. It really works. Just take a piece of bread and toast it until it's black. Then put honey on the toast and eat it. You don't really need the honey but it makes it taste better! It doesn't look good, but it can really help. So if you get stomach ache, try this remedy.

Norma, USA
April 24 9.52

An onion
If you get a high temperature, use an onion. It sounds strange but it helps. Cut one large onion in half and tie half an onion to the bottom of each of your feet. You shouldn't wear socks of course, just bare feet! I use this on my kids and it works every time. The remedy came from a relative from down south.

Heli, Finland
April 23 18.03

A wet teabag
Here are my tips for toothache. You should put a wet teabag on the sore tooth. I always have a wet teabag in the fridge so it's there when I need it. Another idea: take a garlic clove and put it on the tooth. Both these ideas help me nine times out of ten. But if they don't work for you, you should go to a dentist.

Lameed, Egypt
April 23 16.15

Salt water
When I was a child, I got a lot of headaches and my grandmother always did this for me. Put a few drops of warm salt water in your ears. Don't use really hot water. Do this three or four times for both ears. Then lie down and close your eyes for about ten minutes.

---

3 What do you think of these home remedies? Would you like to try them? Why? / Why not?

VOCABULARY
Giving advice

4 a You can use the imperative or *should* to give advice. Complete the sentences with *socks, teabag, water, feet, garlic*.

	✓		✗
You should	Take a _____ clove and put it on the tooth.	Don't	use really hot _____.
	put a wet _____ on the sore tooth.	You shouldn't	wear _____ of course, just bare _____.

b Read to check. **3.32** Listen to the sentences. **P**

You should take a paracetamol and lie down for half an hour.

Is that for a headache?

5 a Think of advice for each of these problems:

a high temperature   headache   stomach ache   backache   toothache

b Talk in groups. Listen to each other's advice and guess the problem.

If you get stomach ache …

GRAMMAR
Giving advice with *if*

1 a Look at the *if* sentences in the table. Then put the words of this sentence in order and add it to the box.

If / an onion / get / a temperature, / you / use .

If + present simple, imperative
If you **get** stomach ache, **try** this remedy.
If you **try** the salt water remedy, **don't use** really hot water.

_____

If + present simple, *should / shouldn't* + infinitive
If they **don't work** for you, you **should go** to a dentist.

You can change the order of *if* sentences:
If you get stomach ache, **try** this remedy. *or* Try this remedy if you get stomach ache.

---

b **3.33** Listen to the sentences. **P**

2 a Match problems 1–6 with advice a–f. There's more than one correct answer.

If you've got a very bad cold, don't go to work.

1	you've got a very bad cold	a	you shouldn't eat a large meal
2	you're allergic to paracetamol	b	be careful what medicine you take
3	your feet hurt	c	don't go to work
4	you've got stomach ache	d	don't go for a run
5	you feel very tired	e	put them in hot water with mustard
6	you've got a problem with your knee	f	you should go to bed early

Grammar reference and practice, R-9

b Now say the six sentences with *if*.

SPEAKING

3 a **3.34** Listen to Amina from Lebanon, Angharad and Nathalie from Switzerland, and Ruth from England talk about their own remedies for a cold. Tick (✓) the remedies they talk about.

- eat oranges   • eat chicken soup   • drink hot honey and lemon juice
- drink black tea with honey   • get on with work   • go to the doctor
- take paracetamol   • inhale steam from hot water

b Read the script on R-17 to check.

4 Talk about these questions in groups.

1   What do you think of their remedies?
2   What do you do when you've got a cold? What about people you know?
3   What's the most popular remedy? What's the most unusual remedy?

" I put my head over a bowl of hot water and inhale the steam. "

12.3 Target activity

Give advice

TASK READING

1 Read the magazine article.
What's the main topic?

a better relationships with colleagues
b a better office environment
c exercising at work

Tips of the week Stay healthy in the workplace

Offices are not always healthy environments. Here are some tips for improving your office and your health.

✓ Try to sit near a window. Natural light makes you feel happier.
✓ Fresh air is good for you, so you should open the window if possible.
✓ If you want to improve the appearance of your office, get some plants.
✓ Get a good chair and make sure the top of your computer screen is at eye level. A bad sitting position can give you headaches and back pain.
✓ Don't sit near an air-conditioner. It dries out your eyes and skin.
✓ If you feel bored, change the colour of your office walls. The right colour improves your mood and helps you to be more creative. White, blue or green offices are better than dark or bright-coloured offices.
✓ Don't use the lift. You should always use the stairs. This keeps you fit.

2 Read the tips again. Find:
- seven things you should do.
- two things you shouldn't do.

3 Do you do any of the things in the article? Why? / Why not?

TASK VOCABULARY
Giving reasons for advice

4 a Cover the article. Complete the sentences with these words.

Fresh air   The right colour   Using the stairs   Plants   Natural light

1 _____ makes you feel happier.
2 _____ is good for you.
3 _____ improve the appearance of your office.
4 _____ helps you to be more creative.
5 _____ keeps you fit.

b Check your ideas in the article.

TASK

5 a You want some advice. Choose one of these topics or use your own ideas.

How to:
○ improve your home cheaply
○ give a talk to a large audience
○ work at home effectively
○ cook a meal for a large group of people
○ entertain a group of children
○ organise a party for 50 people

b You're going to ask for and give advice. Think about how to:
- ask for advice: *I want to improve my home, but I'm not sure what to do.*
- give advice: *You should / shouldn't ...   Don't ...   If you ...*
- give reasons for advice: *Fresh air's good for you.*

6 Ask other students for advice.

7 Did you agree with the advice you got? Why? / Why not?

Keyword *take*

take with nouns

1 a Complete the sentences with these words.

boat trip   message   medicine
photos   tablets

1 OK, and do you prefer taking _____ in a
   drink or tablets? Unit 12
2 Do not take more than four _____ in 24
   hours. Unit 12
3 My mobile phone doesn't take _____ . Unit 3
4 Sorry, he isn't here at the moment ... Can I
   take a _____? Unit 3
5 And would you like to take a _____ on the
   Bosphorus? Unit 2

b You can use take to talk about travel and
medicine. Find examples in 1a. Can you think of
more examples?

2 Can you remember the last time you:

* took a train?
* took a taxi?
* took a message?
* took a really good photo?
* took a trip to somewhere new?
* took a tablet for a headache?

Talk together.

take with time

3 a Underline an activity and circle a time in these
sentences.

1 Travelling home takes a whole day. Unit 7
2 It takes about twenty minutes to walk to the
   centre of Lucknow. Unit 9
3 It takes 50 minutes to travel the nine-mile
   journey across London by unicycle. Unit 9

b Complete these sentences so that they're true
for you. Then compare with a partner.

1 It takes _____ to do my food shopping.
2 It usually takes about _____ to get home
   from work.
3 Starting up my computer takes _____ .
4 It usually takes _____ to cook my dinner.
5 Cleaning my home takes _____ .
6 It takes _____ to read the newspaper.
7 It takes _____ to answer my emails.
8 Flying to Australia takes about _____ .

Independent learning Learning collocations

1 🎧 3.35 Listen to Yukio. What is a collocation?

a   It's a kind of word.
b   It's two words that go together.
c   It's a kind of sentence.

2 🎧 3.35 Listen again. What two mistakes did he make when he first started learning English?
Why did he make them?

3 a When you try to learn new words and expressions, do you write them down?

b Do you write:

a   single words? *watch*
b   collocations? *watch TV, watch films*
c   sentences? *I usually watch TV on Friday evenings.*

4 When you read in English, try to notice and learn new collocations.
Read A–C and find collocations with take, spend, and have.

watch TV **have lunch**
spend money
take a message **go for a walk**
see you soon

A
Too busy?

British actress, Tanya Hoxton, said in an
interview last week that she needs to take
a break. Speaking to *Hello* magazine, she
said she wants to spend more time with
her friends and family. The first thing
she wants to do is have a party for her

B
Stress busting tips for working parents

* Take a break from work. Spend time
  with your kids in the open air – go for
  a walk every day.
* Every few months, let the kids stay
  with their grandparents and have a
  party for your adult friends.

C
HARRY'S BLOG

We had a great party last
weekend to celebrate the
end of the academic year. I
spent a lot of time preparing
for it – more than I did
preparing for exams ...
Anyway, now it's time to
take a break from university
and think about doing some
real work and getting some
money for next term. This
summer, I'm working at

Goal

◉ write an email or note apologising

A

Hi Marc,

I'm writing to say I'm really sorry for not meeting you yesterday. I had a very bad headache and sore throat. I wanted to call you but I haven't got your home or mobile numbers.

I'm really sorry and hope you're not angry with me. Could we meet another time? I promise to be there! And please give me your number!

Write when you have a moment,

Abby

B

Hello Joseph,

Thanks very much for the invitation. I'm very sorry but I don't think I can come. I've got an exam on Sunday (!) so I really should stay at home on Saturday and do some studying.

Thanks again and sorry to be so boring! Hope you have a great time. Let's meet up for coffee some time soon.

All the best,

Abby

C

Hi Mum & Dad,

Hope you had a great holiday, and thanks for letting us stay. Mum, I'm afraid Sammy broke your mug, the one with cats on it. I'm really sorry. I know it was your favourite. Can we buy you another one? Or take you (and dad, of course) out to dinner some time? I'll give you a call at the weekend.

Love, A. xxxxx

1 a What are the names of the people in photos 1–3?
Read A–C to find out.

  b What do you find out about Abby?
Read A–C again and make a list.

  She's studying something.

2 How did Abby say sorry? Cover the emails and notes and match 1–5 with a–e. Then read again to check.

   1 I'm writing to say I'm really sorry for
   2 I'm really sorry
   3 I'm afraid Sammy broke your mug.
   4 I'm very sorry, but
   5 Sorry to

   a I'm really sorry.
   b be so boring.
   c and hope you're not angry with me.
   d not meeting you yesterday.
   e I don't think I can come.

3 When we say sorry, we usually say why. Look at A and B and find out:

   1 why Abby didn't meet Marc.
   2 why Abby didn't phone Marc.
   3 why Abby can't go to Joseph's.

4 Complete the sentences with these words.

   Could   Hope (x2)   Can   Thanks (x2)   Let's

   1 _____ we meet another time?
   2 _____ we buy you another one?
   3 _____ meet up for coffee some time soon.
   4 _____ you have a great time.
   5 _____ you had a great holiday.
   6 _____ very much for the invitation.
   7 _____ again.

5 a Choose one situation for an email.

   It's Sunday afternoon. You have a very bad cold. Tomorrow you have a meeting with a colleague at work, but you think you should stay in bed.

   You're on holiday and you're using your friend's car. Yesterday you had a small accident. You broke one of the lights at the back of the car. Your friend loves his car.

   You visited a friend in another city at the weekend. On Monday morning, you remember that another friend had her birthday party on Saturday.

  b Discuss ideas for your emails in pairs.

   1 Who are you writing to?
   2 How can you say sorry?
   3 What reasons can you give?
   4 Can you use any expressions from 2 and 4?

6 a Work alone and write your email.

  b Look at another student's email. Can you improve your emails together?

7 Read other students' emails. What do you think of their reasons?

Review

VOCABULARY Health and advice

1 **a** Make sentences from the words in the table.

I've got I feel	toothache	a cold
	a sore throat	tired
	a high temperature	stomach ache
	a problem with my knee	sick

b Make sentences giving advice from these words.

You should/shouldn't ...	
go to	a day off work
take	a doctor
eat	work
try	hot lemon juice with honey
drink	black toast and honey
	coffee
	some tablets

c In pairs, take turns to say a problem and give advice. Do you agree with the advice?

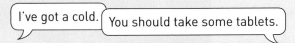

I've got a cold. You should take some tablets.

GRAMMAR Giving advice with *if*

2 **a** Complete the sentences with your own advice.

1 If you like chocolate, ...
2 If you want to buy a new computer, ...
3 If you're looking for a good restaurant, ...
4 If you're interested in films, ...
5 If you need travel information, ...
6 If you'd like to go to a relaxing place, ...
7 If you want to read a good book, ...
8 If you can't sleep well at night, ...

b Compare your sentences. Who has the best ideas?

CAN YOU REMEMBER? Unit 11 – Articles

3 **a** Add *a*, *the* or no article to Holly's story.

> Well, I was in my car in the Rocky Mountains in Canada and I was on ¹_____ highway with lots of beautiful mountains and trees nearby. It was ²_____ sunny day and everything was perfect. Suddenly I saw ³_____ family of bears – ⁴_____ mother bear and two cubs – near the side of ⁵_____ road. I love ⁶_____ bears! So I stopped ⁷_____ car, got out and started taking ⁸_____ photos. I wasn't very close to ⁹_____ bears, but ¹⁰_____ cubs got frightened and ¹¹_____ mother looked angry ...

b Check your answers in ◆3.20 on R-16.

Extension

SPELLING AND SOUNDS *ay, ai*

4 **a** ◆3.36 We usually say *ay* and *ai* in the same way: /eɪ/. Listen and repeat.

day stay way
pain main grain

1 Which spelling is usually at the *end* of a word?
2 Which spelling is usually in the *middle* of a word?

b ◆3.37 Spellcheck. Close your book. Listen to eight words from this unit and write them down.

c Check your spelling on R-17.

NOTICE *it, they*

5 **a** In the first sentence, *it* means 'a piece of bread'. Look at 1–4. Does *it* mean 'honey', or 'black toast with honey'?

> Just take <u>a piece of bread</u> and toast it until it's black. Put honey on the toast and eat ¹it. You don't really need the honey but ²it makes the toast taste better. ³It doesn't look good, but ⁴it can really help.

b Read the advice about toothache. What do *it* and *they* mean in 5–8?

> 💬 I always have a wet teabag in the fridge so ⁵it's there when I need ⁶it. Another idea: take a garlic clove and put ⁷it on the tooth. Both these ideas help me nine times out of ten. But if ⁸they don't work for you, you should go to a dentist.

Self-assessment

Can you do these things in English? Circle a number on each line. 1 = I can't do this, 5 = I can do this well.

⊚ talk about health	1	2	3	4	5
⊚ buy things in a pharmacy	1	2	3	4	5
⊚ understand instructions on medicines	1	2	3	4	5
⊚ give advice	1	2	3	4	5
⊚ write an email or note apologising	1	2	3	4	5

• For Wordcards, reference and saving your work → e-Portfolio
• For more practice → Self-study Pack, Unit 12

13

Experiences

I've never ...

SPEAKING

1 Talk in pairs. When was the last time you:

1 used a mobile phone?
2 went to a gym?
3 worked after eleven at night?
4 read a book you didn't like?
5 saw a horror film?
6 smoked a cigarette?
7 played a new game or sport?
8 ate a hamburger?

READING

2 a Read the web postings.
Are any of them true for you?

File Edit View Favorites Tools Help

Back ✕ ↻ ⌂ 🔍 Search ⭐ Favorites ▶ Media ✉ 🖨 ▭

Address http://www.discussionboard.com

Happy to say, I've never ...

Do you ever feel you're a little bit different from the crowd? What things are you happy you've never done? To post your comment, click here.

I've never had a mobile phone. Why do people these days make phone calls while driving their cars or shopping in the supermarket? When I leave my house, I'm happy to get away from my phone for a few hours!
Frances

I've never read a Harry Potter book or seen any of the films.
Jill

I've never played golf. Why pay money to hit a ball around a large area of land that was once beautiful countryside?
Simon

I've never liked The Beatles. I don't understand people who do.
Maxim

I've never worked for a company with good management. I've never believed managers when they say "people are the most important thing in our company".
Shilpa

I've never smoked, or eaten a McDonald's hamburger.
Marina

I've never wanted to stop smoking.
Thorsten

I've never been to a gym. I've never understood people who climb mountains or do extreme sports!
Denise

I've never said "never"!
Pamela

b Compare your answers.

13.1

GRAMMAR — Present perfect verbs

3 In the article, Frances says *I've never had a mobile phone*. Is she talking about:
1 the past?   2 the present?   3 her whole life up to now?

4 Complete the sentences with 've (have) or 's (has). 3.38 Listen to check.

present perfect (have/has + past participle)
1 I _____ never played golf.
2 You _____ never been to my flat.
3 He _____ never eaten a hamburger.
4 We _____ never had a garden.
5 They _____ never worked in an office before.

5 a Find the past participles of these verbs in the article.

Regular (-ed)
1 play *played*
2 like _____
3 work _____
4 believe _____
5 smoke _____
6 want _____

Irregular
7 go *been*
8 have _____
9 read _____
10 see _____
11 eat _____
12 understand _____
13 do _____
14 say _____

b What are the past participles of these verbs? Look at *Irregular verbs* on p160 to check.

ride take drink fly drive meet be

6 Make sentences with the present perfect.
1 I / never / do / any extreme sports.
2 I / never / understand / maths.
3 We / never / have / a TV at home.
4 My brother / never / smoke.
5 My parents / never / go / to the USA.
6 I / never / be / interested in football.
7 My mother / never / like / cooking.
8 Jo / never / work / in an office before.

WRITING

7 a Write six sentences with never about yourself or people you know, three true and three false.

b Listen to each other's sentences. Which do you think are true? Which are false?

I've always wanted to ...

I've always wanted to swim with dolphins.

I've always wanted to go to Egypt.

LISTENING

1 3.39 Listen to Andrei and Anne talk about things they've always wanted to do. Match the speakers to the pictures.

2 a 3.39 Listen again. Why do they want to do these things?

b Read the script on R-17 to check.

SPEAKING

3 a Think of some things you've always wanted to do.

b Tell each other about the things. Ask questions to find out more.
I've always wanted to ride an elephant. Why?

107

Great places

13.2 goals
- talk about experiences
- talk about places you've been to

**Vocabulary reference
Sights, R-13**

The Winter Palace in St Petersburg is very famous.

1 Which of these things can you see in the town or city where you are now?

a castle   city walls   a fountain   a museum   a palace   ruins   a sculpture   a statue   a tomb   a waterfall   caves   gardens   a skyscraper

2 Talk in groups.

1 Can you think of famous examples of the sights in 1?
2 What kind of sights do you like going to see?

READING

3 What do you know about these places? Have you been to any of them?

Salto Angel, Venezuela

Park Güell, Barcelona

Taj Mahal, Agra

4 a Work in groups of three. A, read about Salto Angel below. B, read about Güell Park on p123. C, read about the Taj Mahal on p127. Find out what these numbers mean.

- **Salto Angel:** 979, 1933, 1937
- **Güell Park:** 60, 1900–1914, 1923
- **Taj Mahal:** 1631, 20,000, 25 million

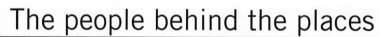

The people behind the places

Salto Angel At 979 metres high, Salto Angel in Venezuela is the highest waterfall in the world. The local Pemon people have always known about the falls and call them Parekupa-Meru (meaning 'waterfall of the deepest place'), but it was a pilot from the USA, Jimmie Angel, who made them famous around the world. He flew over the falls in 1933 and then landed his plane on Aiyan-tepui, the mountain at the top of the falls, in 1937. Later, the falls took his name: Salto Angel in Spanish, Angel Falls in English. They're very difficult to get to, but you can see them from the air or from a boat on the Churun river.

Jimmie Angel

b Tell each other about the people and places.

LISTENING

5 ▶ 3.40 Listen to Monica and Prema talking about the places in the article. Who's been to Güell Park? the Taj Mahal? Angel Falls?

6 a ▶ 3.40 Listen again. Are these sentences true or false?

1 Monica grew up in Barcelona.
2 She thinks Güell Park is beautiful.
3 Prema would like to visit the Taj Mahal.
4 She had a two-week holiday in Venezuela.
5 She saw Angel Falls from a boat.
6 Monica doesn't like flying.

b Read the script on R-17–R-18 to check.

Prema   Monica

7 Which of the places sounds the most interesting? Why?

Have you ever … ?

GRAMMAR
Present perfect

1 a You can use the present perfect to talk about your life up to now. Complete the sentences with **been**, **seen** and **heard**.

present perfect *has* / *have* + past participle
❓ 1   Have you **been** to Güell Park?   ✅ Yes, I have.   2   Have you ever _____ the Taj Mahal?   ❌ No, I haven't.
➕ 3   I've _____ to Angel Falls.   4   I've _____ it on television.
➖ 5   I haven't _____ there.   6   I've never _____ of it.
ever = at any time (in your life)

b 🔊 **3.41** Listen to check. 🅟

2 a Complete the conversations with verbs in the present perfect.

1   **A**   *Have you seen* (you see) the Forbidden City in Beijing?
    B   No, but I _____ (hear) of it.

2   **A**   _____ (you hear) of Petra in Jordan?
    B   Yes, I _____ . Everyone says it's beautiful.

3   **A**   _____ (you eat) sushi?
    B   No, I _____ . What's it like?

4   **A**   _____ (you read) *Anna Karenina*?
    B   I _____ (not read) it, but I _____ (see) a film of it.

5   **A**   _____ (you play) golf?
    B   No. I _____ (see) it on TV, but I _____ (never try) it.

Grammar reference and practice, R-10

b Ask the questions in pairs and answer with your own ideas.

PRONUNCIATION
Linking consonants and vowels 2

3 a Mark the words that link. Remember that consonants at the ends of words link to vowels at the start of words.

1   It's a very unusual place.

2   I've been there lots of times.

3   I've never heard of it. (x2)

4   I've seen it on television. (x2)

5   What's it like?

b 🔊 **3.42** Look at the script on R-18 and listen to check. 🅟 Practise saying 1–5.

SPEAKING

4 a Make a list of:

1   five famous cities around the world.   *Shanghai, New York, …*
2   five cities in the country where you are now.   *Riyadh, Jeddah, …*
3   five places in the town or city where you are now.   *the castle, the Arts Theatre, …*

b In groups, find out who's been to the places on the list. Then use follow-up questions to find out more.

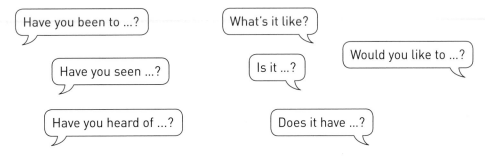

Have you been to …?

What's it like?

Would you like to …?

Have you seen …?

Is it …?

Have you heard of …?

Does it have …?

Get information and recommendations

13.3 goals
◉ talk about experiences
◉ find out information about things

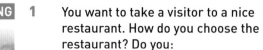

TASK LISTENING

1 You want to take a visitor to a nice restaurant. How do you choose the restaurant? Do you:

- go to a restaurant you know?
- try a new place you've heard about?
- look for places on the internet?
- ask friends about places they know?
- look in a local guide?
- do something else?

2 **3.43** Listen to Kieran asking three colleagues about restaurants.

1 Why does he want to go to a restaurant?
2 Does he choose the Italian, Indian or American restaurant?

TASK VOCABULARY

Getting information

3 **a** Can you remember what they said? Match 1–7 with a–g.

1 Have you been to that new Italian restaurant, Sicilia?
2 You could ask Prema.
3 Have you tried Sicilia, the Italian place?
4 What was it like?
5 It's really nice.
6 Take her to Akash.
7 You'll love it. Really.

a OK, I'll think about it. Thanks.
b No, I haven't, sorry.
c OK, I'll try it.
d OK, I'll ask her. Thanks.
e Akash? I've never heard of it.
f Yes, we went there two, three weeks ago.
g It was OK, but quite expensive.

b **3.43** Listen again to check.

4 In pairs, take turns to say sentences 1–7 and remember the answers.

TASK

5 **a** Choose one situation and think of things to ask about.

You're taking a visitor out for a meal. Think of some restaurants and cafés to ask other students about.

You're thinking about going on holiday somewhere different. Think of some places you've never been to.

You want to do a new sport or activity. Think of some sports and activities you've never tried.

You'd like to do an evening class and learn a new skill. Think of some things you'd like to try.

You'd like to take some interesting books on holiday with you. Think of some books you've heard of, but haven't read.

Have you been to that new Thai restaurant?

No, but have you tried ...?

b Ask other people for information and recommendations.

6 Choose one of the recommendations. Explain why you chose it.

Have you read *One Hundred Years of Solitude*?

Keyword *thing*

1 a Complete the sentences with thing or things.

1 What _____ are you happy you've never done? Unit 13
2 You don't always have time to do all the tourist _____ . Unit 13
3 This is the best _____ … paracetamol. Unit 12
4 The first _____ I saw was a huge spider on the wall. Unit 11
5 Where are the plates and _____? Unit 5

b In which sentences does thing(s) mean *object(s)*? In which sentences does it mean *activities*?

2 a Match 1–6 with a–f.

1 What's that over there?	a Yes. I need to finish a few things before I go home.
2 Are you working late tonight, Chris?	b Yes, I guess we like similar things.
3 Let's go. The next train's at 5.20.	c That thing? It's a unicycle.
4 You and your sister really get along well.	d Not much. Watch TV, read a book, things like that.
5 So, what are we doing today?	e Well, the first thing is, I need to get some money.
6 What do you do on Saturdays?	f OK, I'll just get my things and we can go.

b Cover a–f. Test each other. Take turns to say 1–6 and remember a–f.

3 Find someone in the class who:

1 always has a lot of things in their pockets.
2 has lots of things to do this weekend.
3 likes doing similar things to you.
4 likes cycling and running and things like that.
5 has a lot of things to do at work this month.
6 needs to buy a few things on the way home.

Across cultures Your experiences

1 a 🔊 3.44 Listen to Jessica, David and Hyun talking about their experiences of other cultures. Match each person with a country and a topic.

Egypt Brazil Spain   food people music

b Talk together. What did they say about each topic? Listen again to check.

2 a Match 1–7 with a–g.

1 I was surprised that	a because of the music.
2 It's something people do in Spain	b food.
3 It's more than just	c I've read a lot about it.
4 I remember walking	d on special occasions.
5 I couldn't believe how	e I really enjoyed the food.
6 I got interested in Brazil	f friendly people were.
7 I've never been there, but	g to work for the first time.

b Read the script on R-18 to check.

3 a Think of your experiences of other cultures. For example:

- listening to music or eating food from other countries
- meeting people from other countries
- reading books or watching films from other countries
- going to language classes
- seeing art or cultural exhibitions from other countries
- travelling to another country

b Talk about your experiences with another student.

1 a 🔊 **3.45** Listen to three conversations. Match them with pictures A–C.

b Read conversations 1–3 to check.

2 a Put the highlighted expressions from the conversations into the right groups.

Starting a conversation	Finishing a conversation
How are things?	I'll talk to you later.

b 🔊 **3.46** Listen to check. ⓟ

3 a How can you reply to the expressions in 2a? In groups, think of ideas.

> How are things?

> Fine, thanks.

> I'm great, thanks …

b Compare with the responses in the conversations.

4 a Cover the conversations. Make sentences with these words.

1 Can / talk?
2 Are / doing / anything now?
3 Excuse / got / moment?
4 haven't / seen / long time
5 Have / got / time / a cup of tea?
6 I'll talk / later
7 See / party
8 It / nice talking / you
9 I'll call / time
10 Thanks / help

b In pairs, take turns to say sentences 1–10 and reply.

5 Read the two situations.

1
It's Monday. You phone a friend to talk about your weekend.
1 Say hello and check your friend has time to talk.
2 Ask about your friend's weekend. Talk about your weekend.
3 Finish your conversation.

2
You work for a computer software company. You need to arrange a meeting with your colleague to plan next month's sales conference. Think about when you are free this week.
1 Say hello and check your colleague has time to talk.
2 Agree a day and time for the meeting.
3 Finish your conversation.

Goal

◉ start and finish conversations in different situations

1

SU-MIN	Hello.
KURT	Hello, Su-Min. This is Kurt.
SU-MIN	Oh, hi, Kurt. How are things?
KURT	Fine, thanks. Listen, can you talk now?
SU-MIN	Well, actually, I'm going out in ten minutes. Is it important?
KURT	Erm, no, not really. Can I call you back later?
SU-MIN	Yeah, any time after eight is fine. I'll talk to you later, OK?
KURT	OK, thanks. Bye.

2

JULIA	Abdul … Excuse me, have you got a moment?
ABDUL	Yes, of course.
JULIA	Thanks. I wanted to ask you about the Maxwell account …
JULIA	… well, I shouldn't keep you, Abdul. Thanks for your help.
ABDUL	Any time.
JULIA	Thanks. See you at the meeting.
ABDUL	Yes, see you.

3

ANDREI	Pete! How are you? I haven't seen you for a long time.
PETE	I'm great, thanks.
ANDREI	Hey, are you doing anything now?
PETE	No, not really.
ANDREI	Have you got time for a coffee and a chat?
PETE	Sure, great idea …
ANDREI	… well, it was good talking to you, Pete.
PETE	Yeah, really nice.
ANDREI	Anyway… I'll text you some time.
PETE	Yeah, that would be nice. Take care.
ANDREI	You too. Bye.

6 Have two conversations in A/B pairs. A, start conversation 1. Then, B, start conversation 2.

> Hi, Masha, how are you? Have you got time for a chat?

13 Look again ♻

Review

1 **a** Complete these words with vowels (a,e,i,o,u).

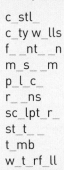

c_stl_
c_ty w_lls
f__nt__n
m_s__m
p_l_c_
r__ns
sc_lpt_r_
st_t__
t_mb
w_t_rf_ll

b Can you see these things in your country? Where? Are any of them famous sights?

c Do you recommend visiting them? Talk together.

GRAMMAR Present perfect

2 **a** Complete the questions with the past participles of these verbs.

buy do eat go meet play read see

1 Who's the most interesting person you've ever _____?
2 What's the worst film you've ever _____?
3 What the most expensive thing you've ever _____?
4 What's the most boring game you've ever _____?
5 What's the most exciting book you've ever _____?
6 What's the most difficult thing you've ever _____?
7 What's the most beautiful place you've ever _____ to?
8 What's the sweetest food you've ever _____?

b Ask and answer the questions together.

CAN YOU REMEMBER? Unit 12 – Health and advice

3 **a** Complete the conversation with these words.

got hear home I'm I've not should to you you

RUUD Are _____ all right?
SALLY No, _____ really. _____ _____ a headache.
RUUD Oh, _____ sorry _____ _____ that. Maybe _____ _____ go _____.

b 🔊 **3.47** Listen to check.

c Think of more expressions for health problems.

a stomach ache, a problem with my knee, ...

d Practise the conversation with different problems and advice. Take turns to start.

Extension

4 **a** 🔊 **3.48** Listen. How do we say wh in each word? Circle /w/ or /h/.

1 what /w/ /h/   6 white /w/ /h/
2 who /w/ /h/   7 wheel /w/ /h/
3 when /w/ /h/   8 whole /w/ /h/
4 which /w/ /h/   9 whisper /w/ /h/
5 why /w/ /h/   10 whose /w/ /h/

b Complete the rule. Then practise saying the words.

Say wh- as /h/ when it is before the letter _____.

c 🔊 **3.49** Spellcheck. Close your book. Listen to ten words and write them down.

d Check your spelling on R-18.

NOTICE both, neither

5 **a** Read part of Kieran's conversation with Monica. Which highlighted word means *Sicilia and Browne's*? Which word means *not Sicilia and not Browne's*?

KIERAN Have you been to Sicilia or Browne's?
MONICA Yes, I have. Both of them.
KIERAN Which one should we go to?
MONICA Neither.

b Complete the conversations with both or neither.

1 **MONICA** So were you on the river or on the mountain?
  PREMA _____. We were in a plane.
2 **HYUN** Most of my CDs are samba and Brazilian jazz. I love _____ kinds of music ...

c Ask and answer questions about pairs of things. Try to use both or neither in your replies.

Have you tried ... ?
Do you like ... ?
Do you use ... ?

> Do you like tea or coffee?
> Neither.
> I prefer tea.

Self-assessment

Can you do these things in English? Circle a number on each line. 1 = I can't do this, 5 = I can do this well.

⊚ talk about experiences	1 2 3 4 5
⊚ say what you've never done and always wanted to do	1 2 3 4 5
⊚ talk about places you've been to	1 2 3 4 5
⊚ find out information about things	1 2 3 4 5
⊚ start and finish conversations in different situations	1 2 3 4 5

• For Wordcards, reference and saving your work → e-Portfolio
• For more practice → Self-study Pack, Unit 13

14 Choices

Exercising your brain

READING

1 What do you think is good for your brain? What's bad for your brain?

> I think sleeping's good for the brain.

2 Read the article about exercising the brain. Were your ideas the same?

Keep your brain in top condition

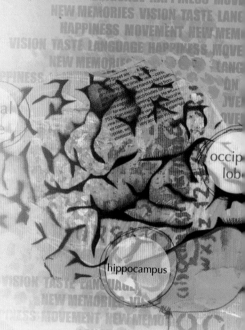

Your brain needs exercise in the same way as your body does. But using your brain doesn't need to be hard work. Have a look at these ideas.

1 Try writing backwards, or writing with your other hand. This makes new connections in your brain and helps you to get new ideas. The great thinker and artist Leonardo da Vinci often used mirror-writing.

2 Start using new parts of your brain. Take up new hobbies, like tennis, chess or dancing the tango.

3 Sleep. If you don't get enough sleep, it's harder for the brain to do some activities, like producing language and new ideas.

4 Chew gum. This exercises the hippocampus, a part of the brain that's important for making new memories.

5 Ask your brain to do old activities in new ways. For example, when you're on a train or bus, close your eyes and guess where you are by listening.

6 Don't eat too much junk food. Cholesterol is bad for both your heart and your brain.

7 Think young! Experiments have shown that when people start to believe they're old, they act old.

8 Play memory games. This keeps your brain young. Games like remembering long lists of words can take ten to fourteen years off the mental age of older people.

9 Learn a new language. This is one of the most difficult things your brain can do, so it's great exercise. It's good for your brain's frontal lobes, which usually get smaller with age.

10 Eat lots of fish. The omega 3 oils in fish like salmon and tuna are good for the brain.

11 Get enough exercise. The right amount of exercise can give people 30% less chance of developing Alzheimer's.

12 Relax. Too much stress is bad for the brain. The hippocampus is about 14% smaller in people who are always stressed.

3 Read again. Why is it a good idea to:

1	write backwards?	5	think young?
2	take up new hobbies?	6	play memory games?
3	get enough sleep?	7	learn a new language?
4	chew gum?	8	relax?

4 Have you tried any of the things in the article? Would you like to try any of them?

Lifestyle choices

VOCABULARY

*too much,
enough,
not enough*

1 **a** Complete sentences 1–4 with too much or enough. Then read the article
to check.

> ***too much, enough* + noun**
> 1 If you don't get _____ sleep, it's harder for the brain to do some activities.
> 2 Don't eat _____ junk food.
> 3 Get _____ exercise.
> 4 _____ stress is bad for the brain.

b Match 1–3 with a–c.

1	enough	a	more than you need
2	not enough	b	what you need
3	too much	c	less than you need

2 🔊 **3.50** Listen to Sue and Dan. Who doesn't get much sleep? Who gets a lot?

3 **a** Can you remember what Sue and Dan said? Add too much, enough and not enough
to the conversation.

SUE Do you think you get _____ sleep?

DAN No, not at the moment, because of the baby. I only slept about four hours last night.

SUE Four hours? Poor you. That's _____ .

DAN What about you?

SUE I usually sleep for about nine hours, probably ten at the weekend. And I'm always tired.

DAN Really? You know, I think that's probably _____ sleep.

b 🔊 **3.50** Listen again to check.

PRONUNCIATION

Review

4 **a** Mark the stress and weak forms in these sentences.

1 Do you think you get enough sleep?

2 No, not at the moment, because of the baby.

3 That's not enough.

4 What about you?

5 And I'm always tired.

b Remember how we link consonants and vowels (get‿enough). Mark the words
that link.

c 🔊 **3.51** Look at the script on R-19 and listen to check. 🅿 Practise saying 1–5.

SPEAKING

5 **a** Think about how much:

- sleep you get
- exercise you do
- fish you eat
- TV you watch
- work you do
- studying you do
- tea or coffee you drink

Is it too much, not enough, or enough?

b Compare your ideas in groups.

> I get about five hours' sleep a night.
>> That's not enough!

Barry Cox

LISTENING

1 Look at the picture and read about Barry Cox. Where's he from? What does he do?

2 a [3.52] Listen to the first part of a radio interview with Barry Cox. Did Barry always want to become a singer? Is he happy with the choices he made?

b [3.52] Listen again. What does Barry say about these things?

1 Spanish lessons
2 a Chinese supermarket
3 a singer from Hong Kong
4 a competition
5 being famous

Barry Cox, an ex-supermarket worker from Liverpool in England, is now a popular singer in China. He sings in Cantonese.

3 Have you ever thought about changing your job or moving to another country?

VOCABULARY

Life changes

4 a What can you remember about Barry Cox? Put these sentences in the right order.

1 I went to a concert given by Leon Lai.
2 I decided to move abroad, to Hong Kong.
3 I had singing lessons.
4 I took up languages.
5 I left school at sixteen.
6 I got a job singing Canto-pop.

b Read the script on R-19 to check.

c Make more expressions to describe life changes. Use the highlighted verbs in 4a and these words.

university (x2)   divorced   a car   a baby
dancing   home (x2)   school   married

went to university

5 a Write six sentences: three things you've done and three things you'd like to do.

I went to university in 1989. I'd like to move abroad one day.

b Compare your sentences with other students.

6 a What do you think Barry Cox wants to do in the future?

• stay in China
• do some travelling
• continue singing
• move to another country
• move back to Liverpool
• learn another language

b [3.53] Listen to the second part of the interview to find out.

Hopes and plans for the future

GRAMMAR

be going to,
be hoping to,
would like to

1 Which sentence from Barry's interview is more certain? Which sentence is less certain?

1 I'm going to stay in China for another few years.
2 I'm hoping to continue with the singing.

2 a Complete the sentences in the table with these words.

I'm   are   He's   I'd   Would   Are

✚	
1 _____ going to	
2 _____ hoping to	stay in China for another few years.
3 _____ like to	

❓	✔ ✖
4 Is he going to stay in China next year?	Yes, he is. No, he isn't.
5 _____ they hoping to move to another country?	Yes, they are. No, they aren't.
6 _____ you like to move back to Liverpool one day?	Yes, I would. No, I wouldn't.
7 What _____ you going to do this weekend?	

b 🔊 **3.54** Listen to check. ℗

3 Look at the game. Write questions with the words on the dark squares.

2 What are you going to do tomorrow?

FINISH

14 What / hoping / do / in the future?

13 Ask a question with *going to*.

12 Would / like / take up / a new hobby?

8 What / going / do / tonight?

9 Ask a question with *hoping to*.

10 Would / like / move / in the next ten years?

11 Start again.

7 Go to square 10.

6 What / going / do / this weekend?

5 Go back one space.

4 Would / like / learn / another language?

START

1 Go forward 2 spaces.

2 What / going / do / tomorrow?

3 Ask a question with *would like*.

Grammar reference
and practice, R-11

4 Play the game in groups.

1 Take turns to throw a coin. For *heads*, move one space. For *tails*, move two spaces.
2 When you land on a square, ask the question or follow the instructions. The other players should ask questions to find out more.
3 If you land on the same square twice, ask another player the question.

Plan a weekend break

14.3 goals
- give opinions
- talk about hopes and plans
- make decisions

TASK LISTENING

1 Look at the tourist information about La Mauricie on the website. Match pictures A–D with a place or activity on the website.

A

B

C

D

http://www.npc.gc.ca/mauricie

LA MAURICIE Canada

▼ **Accommodation**

Camping du Parc ***
We welcome you to Camping du Parc, a friendly campsite close to … *more*

Au Joyeux Druide, Hotel and Art Gallery ***
Our house is on a hill by the Shawinigan River. Here you'll find comfortable rooms … *more*

Le Baluchon ****
Our inn is in a beautiful location near islands, waterfalls, hills and a forest. … *more*

Chalet Joel Migneault **
Rent this warm quiet chalet in the heart of nature on Lake Chrétien. … *more*

▼ **Outdoor activities**

From tree to tree
An extraordinary family activity! Come and experience this new treetop adventure … *more*

Riding Centre, Saint-Georges
Come and enjoy our horses with a qualified instructor. … *more*

Black bear observation
Watch for bears safely with our experienced guides. … *more*

National Park of Canada, Mauricie
A paradise for outdoor lovers with 536 km^2 of lakes and forests. Canoeing and hiking … *more*

2 a 🔊 **3.55** Listen to Dan and Millie planning a weekend in La Mauricie. Tick (✓) the things they talk about on the website.

b 🔊 **3.55** Listen again. Where are they going to:

1 stay?   2 go on Saturday?   3 go on Sunday?

TASK VOCABULARY

Planning

3 a Can you remember Dan and Millie's conversation? Complete the sentences with these words.

expensive   Saturday   nice   accommodation   uncomfortable

Introducing / changing topic	Opinions	Agreeing / disagreeing
What are we going to do about _____ ?	I think it's too _____ .	Yeah, OK. Fine.
What are we going to do on _____ ?	This campsite looks _____ to me.	But camping is really _____ .

b 🔊 **3.56** Listen to check. 🅟

TASK

4 Work alone. You're going to La Mauricie for a weekend with some friends. Look on R-6 and think about:

1 where to stay   2 what to do on Saturday   3 what to do on Sunday

5 Talk in groups and plan what to do.

6 Explain your ideas to other groups. Did you choose the same or different things?

Keyword *really*

really = very

1 a Look at these sentences from previous units. In which sentences can you change really to very?

```
1  But camping is really uncomfortable. Unit 14
2  I really like working with numbers. Unit 7
3  I'm really busy at work. Unit 3
4  I really miss the sun. Unit 2
5  I'm really interested in architecture. Unit 2
6  I really want that coat. It's cold here! Unit 2
```

b Complete the rules with very and really.

You can use _____ with adjectives, but not verbs.
You can use _____ with both adjectives and verbs.

2 a Add really to these questions.

1 Who do you admire?
2 What do you do if you're bored?
3 Do you know a good place to buy gifts?
4 What do you enjoy doing in the evenings?

b Ask and answer the questions.

really = truly

3 We also use really to say or ask if something is true. Match 1–3 with a–c.

1 He says he's a good driver
2 Do you really make
3 People believe jogging's good for you
a all your own clothes?
b but really it's bad for your back and knees.
c but really he's not.

4 a Complete these sentences with your own ideas.

1 A lot of people think … but really …
2 Everyone says … but really …
3 I often think … but really …
4 I sometimes say … but really …
5 My friend believes … but really …

b Compare your sentences with a partner.

> Everyone says English food's awful, but really it's quite nice.

Independent learning How can you learn languages?

a film with subtitles

graded readers

a language exchange

1 **3.57** Listen to Greg from the UK and Paula from Argentina talk about how they learn languages. Circle the things they talk about.

having lessons	reading newspapers or magazines	a discussion group
making friends with local people	reading books	a language exchange
watching films with subtitles	reading graded texts	practising every day

2 a **3.57** Listen to Greg and Paula again. Which methods worked for them? Which methods didn't work? What do they want to try?

b Read the script on R-19 to check.

3 Talk about:

• which methods you've tried for learning English.
• which methods you'd like to try.

Tom   Marek   Jessie

FindOldFriends.com

You can get in touch with old friends on FindOldFriends.com. It's simple. Sign up with us, search for your friends online, then contact them by email.

File Edit View Insert Format Tools Message Help

Hi Marek

I was so pleased when I saw your name on the site! After school, I did a French degree at Liverpool University. After that, I didn't know what to do so I decided to travel. I spent a year in China teaching English, then I moved to the States. Now I'm living and working in LA, managing an internet business. I live alone with my lovely cat, George. In a few years' time, I'd like to get married and have kids, but I haven't found the right woman. Do you remember Jessie Morgan? I always liked her. She was so ambitious at school. I'd love to know what she's doing now. What's your news? It would be great to hear from you.

Tom

1 Look at the website. Have you ever joined a website like this? Which one?

2 Read the emails. Where did Tom, Marek and Jessie become friends? Where are they now?

3 Read again and find out two things:

1 Tom and Marek did in the past.
2 about their lives now.
3 they'd like to do or are planning to do in the future.

4 **a** *Time expressions* Cover the emails. Complete the sentences from Tom's email with these time expressions.

Now   After (x2)   In a few years' time   then

> ¹_____ school, I did a French degree at Liverpool University. ²_____ that, I didn't know what to do. I spent a year in China teaching English, ³_____ I moved to the States. ⁴_____ I'm living and working in LA ... ⁵_____, I'd like to get married and have kids.

b Read the email to check.

c Find and <u>underline</u> similar time expressions in Marek's email.

5 **a** Think of an old friend you last saw at school. Write notes about your life since you saw your friend.

> • left school in 1995   • went to art college

b Tell another student about your life. Decide what time expressions to use.

> After school, I went to art college. Three years later, I ...

Delete Reply Reply All Forward Print

Hi

It's good to hear from you, Tom. After university I decided to go back to Poland and spend some time with my family in Poznan. After a few months, I got a job and moved into a small flat of my own. Ten years later, I've got a great job and a wonderful wife. And you'll never guess who I'm married to – Jessie! We didn't see each other for years after university, but then we got in touch online. She came to see me and we got married last year. We're having a baby next summer and then we're going to move into a bigger place. She's an architect and is doing very well. If you'd like to visit Poland, give us a call. By the way, have you heard from Debbie? Jessie wants to get in touch with her.

Marek

6 **a** Write an email to your old friend. Write about:

- your life since you left school.
- your life now.
- what you'd like to do in the future.

b Exchange emails with a partner. Do you understand everything in the email? Talk about your emails together.

14 Look again ♻

Review

GRAMMAR Hopes and plans for the future

1 **a** 🎧 **3.58** Listen to Khalid talk about his hopes and plans. Tick (✓) the topics he mentions.

studying   children   work   sport
travel   marriage   children

b 🎧 **3.58** Listen again. What are his hopes and plans?

He's going to … He's hoping to … He'd like to …

c Talk in pairs. What are your hopes and plans?

d What do you think are typical hopes and plans for a 20 year-old, a 40 year-old and a 60 year-old?

VOCABULARY Planning

2 **a** Complete the conversation with these words.

enough   too   about   going   OK   looks

JESSIE	So, what are we ¹_____ to do about Marek's birthday?
TOMASZ	Well, we could arrange a big lunch in a restaurant. It could be a surprise.
JESSIE	Yeah, ²_____. Marek would like that. Where?
TOMASZ	Look at this restaurant guide. This place ³_____ good to me.
JESSIE	Hmmm. I think it's ⁴_____ expensive. What about Khan's?
TOMASZ	Yes, that's a good idea. And what are we going to do ⁵_____ invitations?
JESSIE	Well, I haven't got ⁶_____ time to phone everyone …

b Plan a party for someone in the class. Decide what event, what to do and where to go.

c Explain your ideas to the person. Do they like the plan?

CAN YOU REMEMBER? Unit 13 – Present perfect

3 **a** Complete the sentences with your own ideas.

1   When I was younger I didn't like _____, but now I do.
2   I've never liked _____.
3   When I was younger I liked _____, but now I don't.
4   I've always liked _____.

b Talk about your ideas. Are they the same or different?

> When I was younger I didn't like tomatoes, but now I do.

> I've never liked coffee.

Extension

SPELLING AND SOUNDS Silent consonants

4 **a** 🎧 **3.59** Read and listen to these words. Notice that the consonants in red are silent.

could   **k**now   **w**rite   clim**b**   listen

b Work in pairs. Say these words and cross out the silent consonant in each.

talk half would	knee knew	wrong wrist
tomb plumber	two sign	autumn

c 🎧 **3.60** Listen to check. Practise saying the words.

d Spellcheck. 🎧 **3.61** Listen to six words from previous units and write them down.

e Check your spelling on R-19.

NOTICE Gerunds

5 **a** You can use -ing to make nouns from verbs. These are called gerunds. You can use gerunds:

as a subject	Using your brain doesn't need to be hard work.
as an object	Leonardo da Vinci often used mirror-writing.
after prepositions	The hippocampus … is important for making new memories.

Find five more gerunds in the article on p114.

b Complete the conversations with the right words.

1   eat, eating
    A   I don't _eat_ meat at all, only vegetables and things like that.
    B   Why? Is _____ meat bad for you?

2   smoke, smoking
    A   _____ is extremely bad for you.
    B   Well, I only _____ three cigarettes a day.

3   swim, swimming
    A   A lot of people say that _____ is the best exercise.
    B   Maybe, but I can't _____.

Self-assessment

Can you do these things in English? Circle a number on each line. 1 = I can't do this, 5 = I can do this well.

⊚ give opinions	1	2	3	4	5
⊚ talk about hopes and plans	1	2	3	4	5
⊚ make decisions	1	2	3	4	5
⊚ write a letter or email to an old friend	1	2	3	4	5

• For Wordcards, reference and saving your work → e-Portfolio
• For more practice → Self-study Pack, Unit 14

Activities

Unit 11, p91, Getting a flight 5a (Student A)

You work at the airline check-in desk.
Your name is _____ .

Remember that you need to:
- check the passenger's passport.
- give the passenger a boarding pass.
- tell the passenger which gate to go to, and what time they're boarding.

Look at the script on R-16 for language you can use.
Use the information on the 'Departures' board on p90.
Remember that boarding time is normally 40 minutes before departure time.

Unit 13, p108, Great places 4a (Student B)

Antoni Gaudi

Güell Park At the end of the nineteenth century, businessman Eusebi Güell bought a large hill in Barcelona, Spain. The land had no water and not many trees, but Güell asked Antoni Gaudi, an artist and architect, to design and build a small 'city' with 60 luxury houses and a park. From 1900 to 1914, Gaudi created one of the best-known and most unusual parks in Europe, with strange-shaped buildings and colourful sculptures which rise up from the earth. However, only two houses were built and, because Gaudi's style was not fashionable at the time, nobody wanted to buy them. Güell died in 1918 and in 1923 his family gave the park to the city.

Unit 10, p85, Arrangements 3a (Student B)

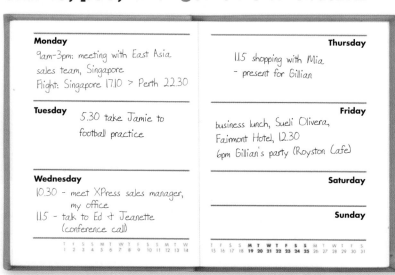

Monday
9am–3pm: meeting with East Asia
sales team, Singapore
Flight: Singapore 17.10 > Perth 22.30

Tuesday
5.30 take Jamie to
football practice

Wednesday
10.30 – meet XPress sales manager,
my office
1.15 – talk to Ed + Jeanette
(conference call)

Thursday
1.15 shopping with Mia
– present for Gillian

Friday
business lunch, Sueli Olivera,
Faimont Hotel, 12.30
6pm Gillian's party (Royston Cafe)

Saturday

Sunday

Unit 8, p67, Friends 2a

How we met

ED SMITH ON VIKRAM SETH

My dad was Vikram's English teacher at Tonbridge School in the 1980s, but the first time I met Vikram was in 1994, just after *A Suitable Boy* came out. He visited Tonbridge to give a reading and stayed the night with our family. I was sixteen and we didn't talk much. He spent most of the time talking to my father.

Six years later, in 2000, we met again in Australia. He was in Perth for work and I was there playing cricket. I rang his hotel and said, "Vikram, it's Edward Smith, Jonathan Smith's son." We met up and spent the afternoon chatting, and had dinner that evening. We talked for hours about books and music. It was wonderful. I'd left university a couple of years before and I missed talking about ideas.

Vikram's a serious person, but he's also great company, intelligent, creative and sometimes very funny. We only see each other from time to time but reading Vikram's books, listening to him, getting to know him – it's all taught me a lot.

1   When did Ed meet Vikram? How old was Ed?
2   Why did Vikram come to Ed's home?
3   When and where did they meet for the second time?
4   How did they spend their time together?
5   What's Vikram like? *He's a serious person, but ...*
6   Do they see each other often?

Unit 8, p69, He's got a beard 3-4a

Discuss and then check your answers on R-5.

Activities

Unit 9, p78, Target activity 4a (Student A)

CONVERSATION 1
You're at the train ticket window in Central Station in Colville. You want to go to Riverton, a nearby town. Ask questions to find out travel details. Buy a ticket.

CONVERSATION 2
You work at the ticket window in a coach station in Albany City. Answer the customer's questions.

Coach ticket: price one way $25.60, day return $45.00, open return $52.75.
Next one leaves in 15 minutes and takes 3 hours 45 minutes; change coaches once. Another one leaves in 30 minutes and takes 3 hours; it's direct. Coach number 613. It's outside, look for sign.

Unit 9, p80, Explore speaking 7a (Student A)

CONVERSATION 1
- You're an employee in a tourist information office. Answer the visitor's questions:
- The Carlton **Inn** is on **Fifth** Avenue. The best way to get there is bus 7. A ticket costs $2.10.

CONVERSATION 2
- You're at a ticket window in a train station.
- You want a single ticket for the 4.40 train to Newmarket Central Station. Ask how long the journey takes.
- Repeat the main points at the end.

Unit 10, p87, Independent learning 3b

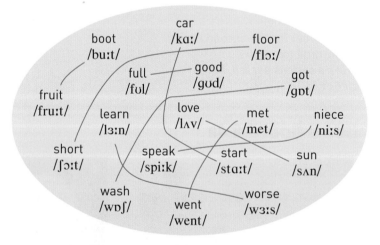

Unit 13, p108, Great places 4a (Student C)

Shah Jehan

Mumtaz Mahal

The Taj Mahal The Taj Mahal is the tomb of Mumtaz Mahal, the third and favourite wife of Shah Jehan, the Moghul emperor of India. When Mumtaz died in childbirth in 1631, the emperor decided to create a beautiful building in memory of his beloved wife, and it took 20,000 workers more than 20 years to complete. The Taj, in the city of Agra on the Yamuna river, is now one of the most famous places in the world: since 2000, it has had more than 25 million visitors. Today Mumtaz and her husband lie in the Taj together, but some people say that Shah Jehan wanted his own tomb to be in a second, black Taj, on the other side of the river.

Unit 11, p91, Getting a flight 5a (Student B)

You work for airport security.

Your name is _____ .

Remember that you have to:
- check the passenger's passport.
- X-ray all hand luggage.
- X-ray shoes.
- check for laptops.
- look in the passenger's bags.

Look at the script on p156 for language you can use.

Unit 11, p93, Telling a story 2a (Student B)

on holiday to France with some friends → get bus and ferry to France → have something to eat in ferry restaurant → fall asleep → wake up in ferry restaurant → my friends not there → ferry empty → at Calais in France → run to bus → too late → see bus driving off ferry ... ?

Think of a good ending for Jack's story. Imagine you are Jack. Prepare to tell the story. Think about:

- the past simple of the verbs (e.g. go > went).
- where to use the (get the bus; the ferry to France).
- where to use storytelling expressions (Later, ...).

Unit 8, p69, He's got a beard 3-4a

Answers
1 1970s, Northern Europe
2 Han Dynasty in ancient China, about 2250 years ago
3 1980s punk fashion, originally UK but popular in other countries
4 early twenty-first century, Nigeria
5 2010, international fashion

Activities

Unit 9, p78, Target activity 4a (Student B)

CONVERSATION 1

You work at the train ticket window in Central Station in Colville. Answer the customer's questions.

Train ticket: price one way $11.00, day return $19.00, open return $25.00.
Next one leaves in 15 minutes and takes 1 hour 10 minutes; change trains once.
Another one leaves in one hour and takes 45 minutes; it's direct. Go to platform 5.

CONVERSATION 2

You're in Albany City at the coach station. You want to go to another city, Kenover, by coach. Ask questions to find out travel details. Buy a ticket.

Unit 9, p80, Explore speaking 7a (Student B)

CONVERSATION 1
– You're in a new city. You're talking to an employee in a tourist information office.
– Ask for the best way to get to Carlton Hotel on Fourth Avenue. Ask how much a ticket costs.
– Check the information at the end.

CONVERSATION 2
– You're selling tickets at a train station. Answer the customer's questions:
– The train leaves at **4.50** and goes to Newmarket **North** Station. The journey takes 45 minutes.

Unit 11, p91, Getting a flight 5a (Student C)

You're the passenger.
Your name is _____ .

Where are you going? Choose a destination from the 'Departures' board on p90. _____
How many pieces of hand luggage do you have? _____
Do you have a laptop in your hand luggage? _____

Look at the scripts on p156 for language you can use.
You need to go to check-in first, then go through security.

Unit 14, p118, Target activity 4

LA MAURICIE Canada

▼ Accommodation

Camping du Parc *
We welcome you to Camping Du Parc, a friendly campsite close to La Mauricie National Park in Quebec, Canada. We offer a quiet site under the trees, a sky full of stars and a good campfire.
On site: a nice little beach, playgrounds, a safe cycling path. Nearby: some golf clubs, many fishing spots, in the heart of La Mauricie.

Au Joyeux Druide, Hotel and Art Gallery *
Our house is on a hill by the Shawinigan River. Here you'll find comfortable rooms, a games room, and good home-grown food. We're also a gallery of modern art.
3573, Rue Bellevue, Shawinigan (Québec)

Le Baluchon **
Our inn is in a beautiful location near islands, waterfalls, hills and a forest. We offer you comfort, a healthy break and excellent food.
3550, Chemin des Trembles, Saint-Paulin (Québec)

Chalet Joel Migneault **
Rent this warm quiet chalet in the heart of nature on Lake Chrétien. On site: hiking, mountain biking, volleyball, swimming, canoeing, kayaking and much more.
496, rue des Peupliers, Saint-Gerard-des-Laurentides (Québec)

▼ Outdoor activities

From tree to tree
An extraordinary family activity! Come and experience this new treetop adventure, unique in Mauricie. Climb trees and cross rope bridges on our specially designed course.
Open: May to October, reservations preferable.
Admission: children: from $16; adults: $25.95; special rates for families and groups.

Riding Centre, Saint-Georges
Come and enjoy our horses with a qualified instructor. Ride alone, in a group or as a family. Ponies available for children. Riding lessons for children and adults.
Open: all year
Rates: adults: $10 / hour; children: $5 / hour; special family and group rates.

Black bear observation
Watch for bears safely with our experienced guides. Learn what to do if you see a bear in the forest! Over 95% of people see bears.
Open: June to September, at sunset.
Rates: adults: $20; students: $10; special family and group rates.

National Park of Canada, Mauricie
A paradise for outdoor lovers with 536 km^2 of lakes and forests. Canoeing and hiking in summer and cross-country skiing in winter are the main activities.
Open: May 12 to October 15, 7 a.m. to 10 p.m.
Admission: $3.50 to $7 per person.

8

Have got

MEANING

Use have got to talk about possessions (things you own), families and appearance.
I've got a silver Toyota.
She's got three children. They've all got blue eyes.

You don't use have got with adjectives, ages or activities.
I'm hungry. ~~I've got hungry.~~
She's 29 tomorrow. ~~She's got 29 tomorrow.~~
I always have lunch in the café next to work. ~~I always have got ...~~

FORM

I, you, we, they	He, she, it
➕ I've got long, brown hair.	➕ He's got three bikes.
➖ We haven't got any children.	➖ The flat hasn't got a balcony.
❓ Have they got a car?	❓ Has she got a computer?
✔ Yes, they have.	✔ Yes, she has.
✖ No, they haven't.	✖ No, she hasn't.

Contractions:
I've got = I have got   He's got = He has got
haven't = have not   hasn't = has not

Have and have got are both common in British English. Have is more common in American English and between international users of English.
Does she have long hair?
(British, American, international English)
Has she got long hair? (British English)

You don't use have got to talk about the past.
I had fair hair when I was a child. ~~I had got fair hair...~~

PRONUNCIATION

You usually contract have got in conversation.
He's got long hair.   They've got a car.

You stress got in positive sentences and questions.
He's got three bikes.   Has she got a computer?
You stress have and got in negative sentences and short answers.
The flat hasn't got a balcony.   Yes, it has. / No, it hasn't.

PRACTICE

1   Complete the sentences with the correct form of have got. Use contractions where you can.

1 He *'s got* long brown hair and he's very tall.
2 They _____ three children and a couple of cats.
3 My flat hasn't got a garden, but it _____ a big balcony.
4 _____ you _____ a bike? We could cycle there.
5 Sorry, I can't read that. I _____ my glasses with me.
6 We _____ a car so we're going by train.

2   Circle the correct expressions. Sometimes both expressions are correct.
1 My cousin has / My cousin's got a small flat in the centre of town.
2 We usually have / We've usually got dinner at six.
3 Does she have / Has she got green eyes like her brother?
4 I'd like to have / have got a shower before we go.
5 When I was a teenager I had / I've got really long hair.

9

COMPARATIVES AND SUPERLATIVES

MEANING

Comparatives
The train is more expensive than the coach.
The train is cheaper than the plane.

Superlatives
The coach is the cheapest way to get to Edinburgh.
The plane is the most expensive.

You use the with superlatives because there can be only one 'best' or 'easiest'.

FORM

Comparatives	Spelling rule	Example
one-syllable adjectives	+ -er + -r if adjective ends in -e	longer safer
one syllable, ending in one short vowel + one consonant	double the last consonant + -er	bigger
two-syllable adjectives	more + adjective	more careful
two syllables, ending in -y	y > + -ier	easier
three syllables or more	more + adjective	more dangerous more interesting
irregular adjectives	good bad far	better worse further

Superlatives	Spelling rule	Example
one-syllable adjectives	+ -est + -st if adjective ends in -e	the longest the safest
one syllable, ending in one short vowel + one consonant	double the last consonant + -est	the biggest
two-syllable adjectives	most + adjective	the most careful
two syllables, ending in -y	y > + -iest	the easiest
three syllables or more	most + adjective	the most dangerous the most interesting
irregular adjectives	good bad far	the best the worst the furthest

PRONUNCIATION

You usually stress more, most and adjectives.
You say –er as /ə/, and –est as /ɪst/.
You don't usually stress than or the. We say them with /ə/.
The train is more expensive than the bus.
You can get the train but it's cheaper to get the bus.
I'm the tallest in my family.
It's the best way to get there.

But when the is in front of a word starting with a vowel, you pronounce it as /ðiː/.
the earliest /ðiː'jɜːliːɪst/, the oldest /ðiː'jəʊldɪst/

PRACTICE

1 Complete the sentences with the comparative form of the adjectives in brackets.

1 Buses in this city are a lot _____ than the underground. (slow)
2 Our new car is much _____ than our old one. (nice)
3 I think that cycling is _____ than driving. (dangerous)
4 Central Market's interesting but it's _____ than Riverside Market. (crowded)
5 Walking's _____ for your health than driving. (good)
6 You can get the bus or a taxi to the station but it's a lot _____ to get a taxi. (expensive)
7 We could go to the cinema but I think the concert looks _____. (interesting)
8 I like walking into town but it's _____ to drive. (quick)
9 The small shops near me are nice but the supermarket's _____ . (cheap)

2 Comparative or superlative? Circle the correct answer in each sentence.

1 I think Rio de Janiero's the most beautiful / more beautiful city in the world.
2 An open return is the most expensive / more expensive than a day return.
3 I love Italian, Chinese and Japanese food but I think Japanese food is the healthiest / healthier.
4 I think driving's the safest / safer than riding a motorbike.
5 This is the biggest / bigger park in my town.
6 I'm the tallest / taller than my brother.
7 In fact, I'm the tallest / taller person in my family.
8 I bought a new computer but it's the worst / worse than my old one.

10
PRESENT PROGRESSIVE – FUTURE ARRANGEMENTS

MEANING

You can use the present progressive to talk about future arrangements, often with a future time phrase.
I'm meeting Jon for coffee this evening.
We're flying to Germany tomorrow.

FORM

See PRESENT PROGRESSIVE, R-11, Combo A.

PRONUNCIATION

See PRESENT PROGRESSIVE, R-11, Combo A.

PRACTICE

1 Complete each sentence with the correct verb in the present progressive.

see go (x2) have (x2) give get (x2) meet work

1 She _____ us at 6.30 tomorrow night in front of Bellini's Restaurant.
2 We _____ to Frankfurt for a conference next month.
3 Sorry I can't come. I _____ late tonight.
4 I think he _____ a taxi to the airport tomorrow morning.
5 I _____ a film with some friends tonight.
6 Professor Hunt _____ a lecture on Matisse this afternoon.
7 We _____ a meeting on Thursday afternoon so don't forget to come.
8 I _____ to the hairdresser's this Saturday.
9 They _____ the 10.30 coach to Seattle.
10 I _____ a party on Friday. Can you come?

2 **a** Put the words in order to make questions.

1 after / are / this class / going / Where / you ?
2 are / getting up / tomorrow / What time / you ?
3 Are / friends / seeing / tonight / you ?
4 are / birthday / How / next / spending / you / your ?
5 are / at / doing / the weekend / What / you ?
6 Are / having / a holiday / in / six months / the next / you ?
7 you / next week / doing / are / What ?
8 soon / you / for food / Are / going / shopping ?

b Ask and answer the questions.

11
ARTICLES

MEANING

Use a/an (indefinite article) when you talk about a person or thing for the first time.
Is there a post office on this street?

Use the (definite article) when the listener knows *which* person or thing you are talking about. For example:
- The listener knows because you talked about it before.
  We've got two cars, a Fiat and a Honda. We use the Fiat to get around the city.
- They know because it's clear from the situation.
  Can you close the door, please?
- They know because there's only one (in the world, or in our situation).
  The sun is really bright today.
  This is why you usually use the with ordinal numbers and superlatives, because there is only one *first* or *best*.
  The first floor   The best cafe   The last time

You don't use an article when you talk about things in general. This is sometimes called zero article.
I don't like coffee. ~~the coffee~~
Bananas are my favourite fruit. ~~The bananas ...~~

FORM

You can use a/an before singular countable nouns.
She's got a boy and a girl.

You can use the before:
- singular countable nouns.
  She's got a boy and girl. The boy's thirteen and the girl's ten.
- plural countable nouns.
  The shops are closed today.
- uncountable nouns.
  Have you got the luggage?

You don't use the with possessives.
This is my uncle. ~~the my uncle~~

You can use zero article before:
- plural countable nouns: *I don't like snakes.*
- uncountable nouns: *I love chocolate.*

PRONUNCIATION

You don't usually stress articles. You say a /ə/ and an /ən/.

You usually say the /ðə/. But when a vowel sound follows the, you pronounce it /ðiː/:
the alphabet   the easiest way   the umbrella

PRACTICE

Add the, a or (–) to these sentences.

1 Look at moon. It's beautiful.
2 Would you like drink?
3 I've got sister and brother. My brother lives in São Paulo and my sister lives in Brasilia. (x2)
4 I love animals.
5 Excuse me, when's next train to Istanbul?
6 This is announcement for all passengers flying to Kuala Lumpur.
7 My brother has got fantastic flat near sea. (x2)
8 Cars are more expensive than motorbikes.
9 Do you prefer tea or coffee?
10 Is there bank near here?

12
GIVING ADVICE WITH *if*

MEANING

You can use if sentences to give advice.
If you get stomach ache, try some black toast.

FORM

If + present simple,	**imperative**
If you get stomach ache,	try some black toast.
If you have a temperature,	don't go to work.
If + present simple,	**should + infinitive**
If this doesn't work,	you should go to a dentist.
If you have a cold,	you shouldn't go to work.

You can change the order. When the *If* part of the sentence is first, put a comma (,) between the two parts.
If you get stomach ache, try some black toast.
Try some black toast if you get stomach ache.

If you have a cold, you shouldn't go to work.
You shouldn't go to work if you have a cold.

PRONUNCIATION

You usually stress if, don't and shouldn't.
If you have a temperature, don't go to work.
If you have a cold, you shouldn't go to work.

You don't usually stress should.
If these remedies don't work for you, you should go to a dentist.

PRACTICE

1   Match sentence beginnings 1–8 with the endings.

1 If your TV doesn't work,
2 You should exercise more
3 Don't forget to take an umbrella
4 If you want a new job,
5 Check a dictionary
6 If you feel stressed,
7 If you want to see him,
8 You shouldn't go to the gym

a) check the adverts in the newspaper.
b) give him a call.
c) if you have backache.
d) call the repairman.
e) you should go for a walk and try to relax.
f) if you want to be fitter.
g) if it rains.
h) if you want to know the meaning of a word.

2   Add the words in brackets to the sentences. Add capital letters and punctuation.

1 Go and see the dentist /ᶦᶠ you have toothache. (if)
2 you want some fruit go to the shop (if, you should)
3 don't eat food with lots of salt you want to be healthy (if)
4 eat a lot late at night you want to sleep well (if, you shouldn't)
5 you go out forget your keys (if, don't)
6 go to bed early you feel tired (if, you should)
7 take these tablets you have a headache (if)
8 check the internet you want travel information (if, you should)

13
PRESENT PERFECT

MEANING

Use the present perfect to talk about experiences up to now, from the past to the present.

| I went to France in 2004. | I went to China in 2007. | I went to India in 2009. |

I've been to France, China and India.

Don't use the present perfect with finished times in the past. Use the past simple.

~~I've been to France in 1990.~~ I went to France in 1990.
~~I've seen Frank yesterday.~~ I saw Frank yesterday.

You can use ever in questions. Ever means 'at any time in your life'.
Have you ever been to France?

FORM

Make the present perfect with have / has + past participle.

I, you, we, they	he, she, it
➕ I've seen all the James Bond films.	➕ She's visited more than twenty countries.
➖ We haven't met Frank. We've never met Frank.	➖ He hasn't been to Japan. He's never been to Japan.
❓ Have they been to Spain? ✅ Yes, they have. ❌ No, they haven't.	❓ Has she met Frank? ✅ Yes, she has. ❌ No, she hasn't.

Contractions:
➕ I've = I have   you've = you have
we've = we have   they've = they have
he's = he has   she's = she has   it's = it has
➖ haven't = have not   hasn't = has not

Most past participles are regular and end in –ed. They're the same as the past simple.
like > liked   smoke > smoked   visit > visited

Some past participles are irregular, but the same as the past simple.
buy > bought   have > had   meet > met

Some past participles are irregular and different from the past simple. They often end with *n*.
eat > ate > eaten   do > did > done   see > saw > seen

Go has two past participles, been and gone.
He's been to India. (= he went to India and he came back)
He's gone to India. (= he went to India and he's in India now)

For past participles, see **Irregular verbs** on R-20.

PRONUNCIATION

You usually stress the past participle. You don't usually stress have / has in positive sentences and questions.
I've seen all the James Bond films.
Has he met Frank?

But you stress have / has in negative sentences and short answers.
We haven't met Frank's wife.
Yes, they have. No, she hasn't.

You usually say been as /bɪn/.

PRACTICE

1 **a Make questions with the present perfect.**
    1 you / go to India?   *Have you been to India?*
    2 you / meet someone famous?
    3 you / have a holiday abroad?
    4 you / swim in the sea?
    5 you / read a book more than once?
    6 you / learn a foreign language apart from English?
    7 your country / win the football world cup?
    8 you / ride a motorbike?
    9 you / do karate or judo?
    10 you / be on a ship?

  b Ask and answer the questions in pairs.

2 **Circle the correct verb in the present perfect or the past simple.**
    1 Have you seen / Did you see Stefan at the party last night?
    2 She's been / She went to Paris six times and now she wants to go again!
    3 I've left / I left university about five years ago.
    4 Where have you been / were you last night?
    5 The first modern Olympics have been / were in Greece in 1896.
    6 The modern Olympics have been / were in Greece twice.
    7 My brother's a journalist. He's visited / He visited a lot of countries.
    8 My great-grandfather was a journalist. He's visited / He visited a lot of countries in the 1890s.
    9 I never / have never smoked.
    10 I started / have started school when I was five.

14
FUTURE – *be going to, be hoping to, would like to*

MEANING

You can use be going to when you talk about future plans.
I'm going to start a new course soon. I paid for the first month yesterday.

You can use be hoping to when you talk about hopes for the future. It is less certain than *be going to*.
I'm hoping to go to university next year. I've got an interview next week.

You can use would like to when you talk about what you want in the future.
I'd like to go to Japan one day.

FORM

be going to, be hoping to + infinitive

⊕
I'm going to start university next year.
I'm hoping to move abroad one day.

⊖
I'm not going to start university next year.

❓
Are you going to start university next year?
✔ Yes, I am. ✘ No, I'm not.
Is he hoping to start his new job next week?
✔ Yes, he is. ✘ No, he isn't.
What are you going to do next weekend?

would like to + infinitive

⊕
I'd like to start university in September.

⊖
I wouldn't like to work abroad.

❓
Would you like to go to university one day?
✔ Yes, I would. ✘ No, I wouldn't.
What would you like to do with your life?

PRONUNCIATION

You can say going to as /ɡəʊntə/ or /ɡəʊɪntuː/.
In fast speech, people often say /ɡənə/.

In positive sentences and questions, you don't usually stress the auxiliary verb (be or would).
I'm hoping to move abroad next year.
Are you going to move abroad next year?
I'd like to start university in September.

In negative sentences and short answers, you usually stress the auxiliary verb (be and would).
We aren't going to have a holiday this year.
I wouldn't like to go to university.
Yes, I am. No, I wouldn't.

PRACTICE

1 Complete the sentences with be going to and the correct verb.

~~do~~ finish go stay change ask visit make

1 "Did they clean the car?"
  "No, but they *'re going to do* it this afternoon."
2 "Have you ever been to India?"
  "No, but I _____ next year."
3 "How's your new job?"
  "I don't like it. I _____ jobs
  again soon."
4 "Did she finish the report?"
  "No, she _____ it tomorrow."
5 "Is dinner ready?"
  "No. I _____ it now."
6 "Can Sam come to the park later?"
  "No. He _____ at home and study."
7 "Did you ask Jessie to come to the party?"
  "No. I _____ her tonight."
8 "What are your plans for the summer?"
  "Oh, we _____ relatives in
  New Zealand."

2 **a** Put the words in the right order to make questions.
  1 which / country / would / you / visit / most like to?
  2 most like to / which / person / would / you / meet?
  3 do / what / are / you / next summer / going to?
  4 learn / you / hoping to / are / one day / another
    language?
  5 like to / would / another country / you / live or work /
    in / one day ?
  6 are / what / you / hoping to / in the next five or ten
    years / do?
  7 are / you / what / do / at work or school / in the near
    future / going to?
  8 would / what / buy / like to / soon / you ?

  b Ask and answer the questions.

Vocabulary reference

8 Family

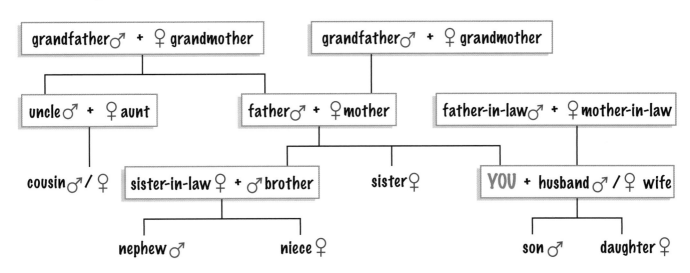

8 Personality

adventurous /əd'ventʃ°rəs/ *adj*
liking to try new or difficult things:
I'm going to be more adventurous with my cooking.

creative /kri'eɪtɪv/ *adj*
good at thinking of new ideas and making interesting things: *Her book is full of creative ways to decorate your home.*

funny /'fʌni/ *adj* **1** making you smile or laugh: *a funny story*
2 strange or unusual and not what you expect: *This chicken tastes a bit funny.*

hard-working /hɑːd'wɜːkɪŋ/ *adj*
doing a job seriously and with a lot of effort: *She's a very hard-working student.*

independent /ˌɪndɪ'pendənt/ *adj*
not wanting or needing anyone else to help you: *She's a very independent four-year-old.*

intelligent /ɪn'telɪdʒ°nt/ *adj*
able to learn and understand things easily: *She is a highly intelligent young woman.*

outgoing /aʊt'gəʊɪŋ/ *adj* Someone who is outgoing is friendly, talks a lot, and enjoys meeting people.

serious /'sɪəriəs/ *adj*
A serious person is quiet and does not laugh often: *a serious child*

8 Independent learning 4a

necklace /ˈnekləs/ *noun*
a piece of jewellery that you wear around your neck: *a pearl necklace*

exhibition /ˌeksɪˈbɪʃᵊn/ *noun*
when things such as paintings are shown to the public: *There's a new **exhibition of** sculpture on at the city gallery.*

traditional /trəˈdɪʃᵊnᵊl/ *adj*
following the customs or ways of behaving that have continued in a group of people for a long time: *traditional farming methods*

image /ˈɪmɪdʒ/ *noun*
1 the way that other people think someone or something is: *They want to improve the **public image of** the police.*
2 a picture, especially on film or television or in a mirror: *television images of starving children*
3 a picture in your mind: *I have an **image of** the way I want the garden to look.*

fashionable /ˈfæʃᵊnəbl/ *adj*
popular at a particular time: *fashionable clothes*

From *Cambridge Essential English Dictionary*

12 The body

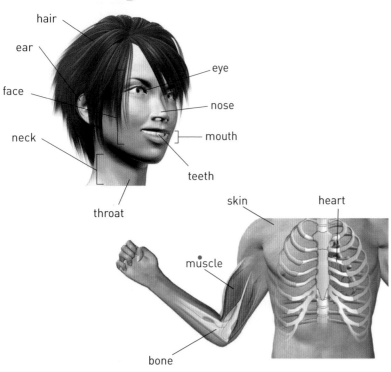
hair
ear
face
neck
eye
nose
mouth
teeth
throat

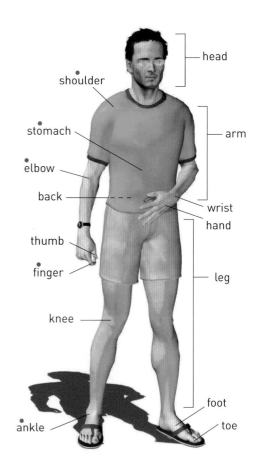
head
shoulder
stomach
elbow
back
thumb
finger
arm
wrist
hand
leg
knee
foot
toe
ankle

skin
heart
muscle
bone

13 Sights

 a castle
 city walls
 a fountain
 a palace
 ruins
 a sculpture

 a statue
 a tomb
 a waterfall
 caves
 gardens
 a skyscraper

🎧 2.35

MALE: brother, father, dad, grandfather, nephew, son, uncle.
FEMALE: aunt, daughter, grandmother, mother, mum, niece, sister.
BOTH: child, children, cousin, parents, twins.

🎧 2.36

PART A

ONYINYE   People say I have a large family but I don't think I have. There are seven people in my family. I have four sisters, so five girls, and then my mum and my dad. But most of my family live in Nigeria. And, erm, my uncle and aunt, for example, they have nine children or eight children. So my family with five children is not really a large family!
CHIE   Oh not really, no.
O   But, erm, here people say that five girls is a large family.
C   Yes.
O   Yeah.

PART B

ONYINYE   I'm lucky because I live with my sister, so I see, I see her a lot of the time.
CHIE   That's nice.
O   And I see my parents quite often as well but, erm, they don't live in the neighbourhood but they live in another part of England.

PART C

ONYINYE   The member of my family that I'm closest to is my sister. And it's funny because I'm thirty years old and she's twenty years old but, erm, our mum says we're like twins, just born ten years apart. We look very similar and, er, we have similar style, we like similar things, so that's why I'm the closest to her.

🎧 2.37

most of my family   a lot of the time

another part of England

a member of my family

🎧 2.39

1 Have you got glasses?
2 Yes, I have. / No, I haven't.
3 They've got pale skin.
4 I haven't got a lot of jewellery.
5 Has she got a tan?
6 Yes, she has. / No, she hasn't.
7 She's got a *bindi*.
8 He hasn't got a beard or moustache.

🎧 2.40

LESLEY   Well, one person I really admire is my neighbour Sybil. Er, she's Scottish and she's in her eighties so she doesn't go out much now, er, but she's very outgoing and loves talking – in fact, er, she sometimes talks too much but that's OK. We don't see each other a lot ... we have coffee together maybe once or twice a month. We get on really well, I guess because we're interested in the same things, like books and food.

Er, she lives alone. Her husband died a few years ago. She's got a daughter who lives in another city and the daughter keeps asking her to go and live with her but Sybil says no every time. She's very independent and I think she loves her own flat and her own, you know, quiet life.

Anyway, once, when I was at her flat, I noticed a silver cup and a photo of her in an old-style sports car. I found out that when she was younger, she was very adventurous and even got into car racing! Her uncle was a rally driver and he trained her for the Ladies Hillclimb Championship race. For this race, they had to drive their cars up a mountain road to the top as fast as possible, and she actually won the race! She was beautiful then ... and she still is now ... very slim, always in perfect clothes. Er, her hair's silver but she's got bright blue eyes. It's hard to imagine she's over eighty, but she is. I think she's great.

🎧 2.41

1
We don't see each other a lot.
We get in touch maybe twice a year.
We spend a lot of time together.
2
We get on really well.
We can talk about everything together.
We're very close.
We don't know each other very well.
3
We're interested in the same things.
We like different things.

🎧 2.42

One is /θ/ in *thanks*.
Two is /ð/ in *brother*.
Three is /ʃ/ in *short*.
Four is /ʒ/ in *usually*.
Five is /tʃ/ in *children*.
Six is /dʒ/ in *jewellery*.
Seven is /ŋ/ in *outgoing*.
Eight is /j/ in *yellow*.

🎧 2.43

alphabet   because   next   office
together

🎧 2.46

1 each   2 niece   3 jeans   4 agree
5 team   6 free   7 believe   8 teacher
9 green   10 reading

🎧 2.47

1 get the underground
2 get the bus
3 get the train

4 cycle
5 ride a motorbike
6 get a taxi
7 drive
8 walk

🎧 2.48

MEERA   Morning, Vijay.
VIJAY   Good morning!
M   Sleep well?
V   Yes, thanks. Ah, tea ...
M   So what are we doing today?
V   Well, could we go and have a look round the city? It's so interesting to see a new place.
M   Sure, good idea.
V   Actually, the first thing is I need to get some money. Is there a cash machine near here?
M   No, but there are a couple next to Halwasiya market, in Hazratganj.
V   Erm, where's that? In the centre?
M   It's the main shopping area, yes.
V   All right. And another thing ... are there any bookshops here? English bookshops?
M   Ha! Are you bored?
V   No, of course not, but you know I like reading and I didn't bring any books because they're so heavy.
M   OK. The best bookshop is Universal Booksellers. That's in Hazratganj too.
V   Great. Do you know when it's open?
M   I think it opens at ten or ten-thirty and closes around eight-thirty.
V   OK, so what's the best way to get there? Can we walk?
M   Well, we could but it's hot and quite crowded.
V   How long does it take?
M   About twenty minutes.
V   Hm. Is there a bus?
M   Not from here, no. It's better to get a taxi ... or we could get an auto.
V   An auto?
M   I mean an auto-rickshaw.
V   OK, good idea. Where's the nearest rickshaw stop?
M   There isn't a stop. We just have to walk until we see an auto and then stop it.
V   OK.

🎧 2.49

1
A   Where's the nearest bus stop?
B   It's on Station Road.
A   What's the best way to get there?
B   Oh, you can walk.
A   How far is it?
B   About half a kilometre.
2
A   Is there a bank near here?
B   Not really. The nearest one is next to the train station.
A   Is there a bus?
B   It's better to get the metro.
A   How long does it take?
B   About fifteen minutes.

Scripts

3

A Er, where can I buy some shoes?
B The best shoe shop is Porter's.
A Is it far?
B No. It's a ten-minute walk.
A What time does it open?
B It opens at nine-thirty.

2.50

quick, quicker, the quickest
safe, safer, the safest
long, longer, the longest
careful, more careful, the most careful
crowded, more crowded, the most crowded
dangerous, more dangerous, the most dangerous
easy, easier, the easiest
good, better, the best
bad, worse, the worst
far, further, the furthest

2.51

ASSISTANT Can I help you?
VIJAY Yes, I want to go to Basingstoke today. How much does a return ticket cost?
A A day return or an open return?
V Erm, what's the difference?
A Well, the open return's more expensive, but you can come back any time. With a day return, you come back today.
V Right ... how much does an open return ticket cost?
A To Basingstoke? It's £15.45.
V And what time does the next coach leave?
A It leaves at 4.15, in fifteen minutes.
V Is it direct?
A No. You need to change coaches once, so it's quite slow ... but the 4.30 coach is direct.
V Oh, that's good. How long does it take to Basingstoke?
A The direct coach? About an hour and a half.
V All right. I'd like an open return ticket on the direct coach, please.
A Thank you ... here's your ticket and change.
V Thanks. Er, which coach do I get? The number?
A Number 342.
V OK, and where do I get it?
A Just outside those doors. You'll see the sign.
V OK, thanks a lot.

2.52

MARIKE One of the best things about Amsterdam is we don't have a big car culture. In fact, the government here thinks about public transport and bicycles first, and cars second. I think that's different from many other countries. People say Amsterdam's a centre of bicycle culture and, erm, that's true. I mean, we have about 400 kilometres of bike lanes. And also, we have bike traffic lights. They look the same as traffic lights but they, erm, they have the shape of a bicycle. Do other countries have those? I don't know. Anyway, some streets don't have bike lanes but you can cycle on them and cars will go around you or follow you. As I said, we're really bicycle-friendly.

HASAN In Dubai, everyone I know uses a car. They're cheap because they're tax free and petrol's not too expensive ... well, actually, prices are going up. We also use taxis a lot but it's harder to find a taxi than before. There aren't enough these days. There are some buses, too, but it's easier and people really love their cars. They're air-conditioned, quiet and private ... Of course the roads in Dubai are very crowded, but we have a new metro now so maybe that will change things. But if you want to go to the desert or mountains or to, say, Abu Dhabi, the car's the best way. We have great roads.

2.53

VIJAY Hello?
SARA Vijay, hi. It's Sara.
V Oh, hi. How are you?
S Great. What about you?
V Yeah, good.
S Listen, do you want to meet up soon?
V Yeah, when? This week?
S Yeah! Thursday? Or Friday?
V Well, Thursday's a problem but I'm free on Friday.
S OK, Friday. Why don't we go out for dinner?
V OK.
S Do you know a good place?

2.55

1 SARA Was that Campie Street? P for Peter?
2 VIJAY No, Cambie Street. B for Bob.
3 V Sorry, not the Palace Theatre. I mean the Royal Theatre.
4 S Sorry, is that 393 or 353?
5 V Well, it's not next to the theatre, exactly. It's near it.

2.56

1 sweeter 2 shortest 3 funny
4 getting 5 meeting 6 swimming
7 moving 8 sitting 9 planned
10 driver

3.2

MIA Some of these films look quite interesting.
JON Yeah. Why don't we go and see one some time this week?
M Yeah, OK. Would you like to see *Family Law*? I heard it's really good.
J Hm, I don't know. It sounds a bit boring. We could see *The Others*.
M Well, I don't usually like horror films, but that one sounds good.

3.3

KIMIKO Hi Jon.
JON Hi! Kimi, what happened?
K I was stuck in traffic and then I got a phone call from my boss. I told you it was a difficult day.
J Yeah, you did. Well, we're walking to Delmonico's now for a pizza. Can you join us?
K Thanks, Jon, but I feel really tired. I think I'll stay at home.
J Are you sure?
K Yeah, sorry.
J OK. Well, erm, how about on Friday?
K Sorry but I'm flying to Singapore this Friday.
J You're not going for work, I hope.
K Yep, for a sales meeting.
J So when are you back?
K Er, it's only a short trip. I'm coming back on Monday night. I'll call you for a chat tomorrow, OK?
J OK, well, have a good evening.
K Thanks, Jon, and enjoy your pizza. And say hi to Mia.
J Will do. Bye now.
K Bye.

3.5

a coffee break | a yoga class |
a guitar lesson | a tennis match |
a cinema programme

3.6

REETA Listen, erm, I have no plans for this weekend so would you like to come over to my place and watch a film?
JANE Well, yeah, that sounds great. Which day?
R Er, how about Saturday night?
MATTHEW Sorry, I'm going out on Saturday. What about Sunday?
R Fine with me. Jane?
J Yeah, that sounds good.
R OK, then why don't you come over at 6.00 and we can have pizza first.
M Great.
R Great. So, do you want to bring a film? Or I can rent something ...
M Erm, how about *The Bourne Supremacy*?
J What's it like?
M Well, it's an action film, I guess. It's about an American spy who loses his memory.
J Oh, right. Who's in it?
R Matt Damon.
M Yeah, that's the one.
J Hm, I don't really like action films.
R OK. Then let's watch ... erm ... *Pan's Labyrinth*.
J *Pan's Labyrinth*? Sounds unusual. What's it about?

R It's about a young girl and it's set in Spain ... in the 1940s, I think. It's really good.

M Hm.

R Matthew's not sure.

M No ...

J I've got an idea. I read about this film called *Yeelen* ...

R *Yeelen*?

J Yeah, it's from Mali, I think. It's about this young man with magical powers.

M That sounds interesting.

J Yeah, I'd really like to see it.

R OK, I'll try to get it. How do you spell the title?

3.7

1 A You look stressed. Is there a problem?
  B Yes, there is! Do you know anything about computers?

2 A Can I see the room this evening?
  B Sure. How about six thirty?

3 A Do you know that Dave's getting married?
  B Yes, I heard about that.

4 A Don't forget the party on Friday.
  B What party? No one told me about that.

5 A Hello, can I help you?
  B Yes, please. I have a question about my ticket.

6 A How was your day?
  B It was terrible! I don't want to talk about it.

7 A So, do you want to buy these jeans?
  B Hmm. I don't know. I'll think about it.

3.8

1 Yuri Gagarin went into space in 1961.
2 An adult elephant has 24 teeth.
3 The first modern Olympics were in 1896.
4 Mount Everest is 8,848 metres high.
5 There are 11 people in a cricket team.
6 The Great Wall of China is about 6,500 kilometres long.
7 It takes 8 minutes and 18 seconds for light to travel from the sun to the earth.
8 People started writing about 5,000 years ago in Mesopotamia.

3.9

1 is /æ/ in *black*.
2 is /ɑː/ in *park*.
3 is /e/ in *help*.
4 is /ɜː/ in *first*.
5 is /ɪ/ in *six*.
6 is /iː/ in *meet*.
7 is /ɒ/ in *lot*.
8 is /ɔː/ in *sport*.
9 is /ʌ/ in *but*.
10 is /ʊ/ in *good*.
11 is /uː/ in *food*.
12 is /ə/ in *sister*.

3.10

1 horror 2 morning 3 comedy
4 beautiful 5 mother 6 moustache

3.11

SUZI So Michelle, do you have any plans for tomorrow?

MICHELLE Hm, not really. Why don't we go to Heidelberg?

S That sounds good. We could do some shopping.

M Hm, I don't know. Let's visit the castle.

S All right. But I need to buy a coat.

3.13

1 good 2 page 3 message
4 great 5 dangerous 6 religion
7 girl 8 arrangements 9 together
10 colleague 11 engineer 12 Egypt

3.14

BELINDA Good morning.

CHECK-IN ASSISTANT Good morning, madam. Tokyo?

B That's right.

C Can I see your passport, please?

B Here you are.

C That's fine. Do you have any hand luggage?

B Just this bag.

C Did you pack your bag yourself?

B Yes, I did.

C Are you carrying anything for anyone else?

B No.

C Right, thank you. Here's your boarding pass. Boarding is at 11.55 from gate 20.

B Thanks.

C Enjoy your flight.

3.15

1 Can I see your passport, please?
2 Do you have any hand luggage?
3 Did you pack your bag yourself?
4 Are you carrying anything for anyone else?
5 Boarding is at 11.55 from gate 20.

3.16

OFFICER 1 Keys?

BELINDA I've put them in my bag.

O1 OK. Is there a laptop in here?

B No.

O1 And your shoes, please.

B Oh, OK.

OFFICER 2 Come forward, please.

B Oh, I'm so sorry.

O2 Keys? Wallet?

B Uh, they're in my bag.

O2 Mobile?

B That too.

O2 Are you wearing a belt?

B Oh yes, sorry.

O2 That's fine, thank you.

B Thanks.

  ...

OFFICER 3 Could you open your bag, please?

B OK.

O3 That's fine. Enjoy your trip.

B Thanks.

3.18

1 When was the last time you saw a spider?
2 Do you like pasta?
3 Is there an art gallery near here?
4 Can you open the door, please?

5 Have you got a pen I can use?
6 What's the name of the person next to you?
7 Do you like cats?
8 What's the easiest language to learn?

3.19

1 **To start a story:**
It was two in the morning.
I was with some friends.
Well, this was a few weeks ago.

2 **To link a story:**
Later, ... and then, ...
After that, ...

3 **To end a story:**
It was really strange.
I had a great time.
In the end, ...

3.20

HOLLY Well, I was in my car in the Rocky Mountains in Canada and I was on a highway with lots of beautiful mountains and trees nearby. It was a sunny day and everything was perfect. Suddenly I saw a family of bears – a mother bear and two cubs – near the side of the road. I love bears! So I stopped the car, got out and started taking photos. I wasn't very close to the bears but the cubs got frightened and the mother looked angry. She started walking towards me. I ran back to the car but I couldn't open the door and the keys were inside. I was really frightened. The mother bear came closer. Suddenly a big tour bus drove up and stopped. The bears ran into the trees. The driver shouted at me, 'Never, never get out of your car when you see bears! They're not pets, they're dangerous!' He and a passenger opened the car door for me and I thanked them and left. That was a real lesson for me.

JACK Well, this was a couple of years ago. I went on holiday to France with some friends. We got the bus and the ferry to France and had something to eat in the ferry restaurant. Then I fell asleep. Later, I woke up in the ferry restaurant but my friends weren't there. The ferry was empty! We were at Calais in France. I ran to the bus but I was too late. I saw the bus driving off the ferry. So I walked off the ferry and phoned my friends. They were all on the bus. We arranged to meet in Paris later that day so I got a train to Paris. It was a terrible journey, but in the end it was OK because I met a really nice Frenchman, Charles, on the train. We're still friends today.

3.21

SAM I was in London at the time and wanted to go to Dublin in Ireland to see my friend, Margaret. This was last year ... and I had to get up really early to catch the plane. The flight was at five in the morning or something. So I got up in the dark and drove to the airport, only to see that my flight was cancelled. There wasn't another flight that day or night, so I booked a seat for early the next morning. I spent all day and all night at the airport. It was so boring! At around midnight I tried to sleep on some free seats but it was really uncomfortable so in the end I stopped trying. I was really tired and in a very bad mood by the next morning. The plane finally took off at nine o'clock but then an hour later they said the plane couldn't land in Dublin and we had to go to Cork, in the south of Ireland! Anyway, I met a lot of really nice people during the journey. We stayed in a lovely five-star hotel in Cork, paid for by the airline, and we had a lot of fun that night. My friend came to get me in her car the next day and it was fine. It was a terrible journey but I also had a really great time.

3.22

1 He drove to the airport.
2 The flight was cancelled.
3 He booked a seat on another flight.
4 He spent all night at the airport.
5 The airport was uncomfortable.
6 He caught the plane to Dublin.
7 The plane took off at nine o'clock.
8 It had to go to Cork in the south of Ireland.
9 He stayed in a five-star hotel.
10 He had a great time there.

3.25

/ŋ/ skiing long running thing
/ŋg/ longer stronger youngest

3.26

1 longer   2 flying   3 youngest
4 thing   5 skiing   6 long

3.27

1 Your head weighs about 5.5 kilos.
2 The stomach can hold 4 litres of food.
3 You use 12 muscles to smile. You use about 70 muscles to speak.
4 Our eyes never grow. Our nose and ears never stop growing.
5 The body loses more than half a kilo of skin every year.
6 Over 50% of the bones in your body are in your hands and feet.
7 The smallest bone is in your ear. It's the size of a grain of rice.
8 Your thumb is the same length as your nose.
9 Children have 20 first teeth. Adults have 32 teeth.
10 Your heart beats about 100,000 times every day.

3.28

A I've got a pain in my back.
B I've got a sore throat.
C I've got a temperature.

D I've got a problem with my knee.
E I've got a headache.
F I feel sick.
G I've got a cold.
H I feel tired.

3.29

PHARMACIST   Hello. Do you need any help?
MARC   Yes. Er, I need something for … well, I guess for pain.
P   OK, what are your symptoms?
M   I've got a pain in my back and I've also got a headache, but that's all.
P   How long have you had the symptoms?
M   The back pain started last night and I've had the headache for about an hour.
P   OK. There are a few things you can try. Are you allergic to anything?
M   Just dairy products.
P   Are you taking any other medicine?
M   No, not at the moment.

3.30

PHARMACIST   OK, and do you prefer taking medicine in a drink or tablets?
MARC   Tablets, please.
P   This is the best thing … paracetamol. It's for all aches and pains. So it has everything you need.
M   All right.
P   Don't take any other painkillers with paracetamol, nothing. You mustn't take anything else.
M   Yes, OK.
P   And if they don't work in a day or two, you should go to the doctor.
M   All right. Thank you.

3.33

If you get stomach ache, try this remedy.
If you try the salt water remedy, don't use really hot water.
If you get a temperature, use an onion.
If they don't work for you, you should go to a dentist.

3.34

ANGHARAD   If I have a cold, I usually take medicine like aspirin or I put my head over a hot bowl with hot water and inhale the steam.
AMINA   Really? My mother and my grandmother do that, but I think, I don't really do that. When I've got a cold, I either go to the doctor, or I just try and ignore it, and just get on with my normal work.
RUTH   My grandmother told me that if you drink hot honey and lemon juice, it's the best cure for a cold, but I'm not sure if that's true. I prefer paracetamol.
NATHALIE   Yes, me too. That's … my mother always tells me to drink black tea with honey too, and to eat soup because you're not very hungry when you have a cold.
AMINA   Hmm. My mum always makes chicken soup when I've got a cold. It's the best thing.

3.35

YUKIO   OK, collocations are words that go together. You see them and hear them everywhere, the same expressions again and again. Like, in English, we say *watch TV* and *spend money*, for example, but, erm, when I first started learning English, I said *see TV* and *use money*. And the reason was that in Japanese, our collocations are *see TV* and *use money* – so I just translated them and thought they were OK … but they weren't. So I think it's important to learn collocations, you know, words that go together … and not just single words. It helps you speak more naturally.

3.37

1 Saturday   2 way   3 waiting
4 explain   5 play   6 saying
7 emails   8 holiday

3.38

1 I've never played golf.
2 You've never been to my flat.
3 He's never eaten a hamburger.
4 We've never had a garden.
5 They've never worked in an office before.

3.39

ANDREI   Well, I've always wanted to go to Egypt …
ANNE   OK.
ANDREI   … to see the, er, pyramids. I've read so many books about them and I just want to see them in real life. I've never been there. I just want to go inside a pyramid.
ANNE   Why do you like the pyramids?
ANDREI   I don't know, when I was a child I thought they were great and you read stories about them and you imagine what they're like. I've always wanted to go, yeah.
ANNE   Maybe you will, one day.
ANDREI   Maybe one day, yeah. What about you?
ANNE   Erm, I've always wanted to swim with dolphins.
ANDREI   Dolphins?
ANNE   Dolphins. Er, many, many years ago I went on holiday to Scotland and I went on a boat trip …
ANDREI   OK.
ANNE   … and we saw some dolphins and they were swimming next to the boat and it was absolutely fantastic.
ANDREI   Dolphins in Scotland?
ANNE   Yes. Unfortunately I couldn't jump in the water but because of that I've always wanted to swim with dolphins. Somewhere warm would be best.

3.40

PREMA   Monica, have you been to, er, Güell Park?
MONICA   Güell Park.
P   Güell.
M   Yes, of course. It's a very … unusual place.

P But you're not from Barcelona?
M No, I grew up in Pamplona ... but I've been to Barcelona lots of times. I have family there.
P Right. Anyway, I've never heard of this park. It sounds beautiful.
M Well, I don't think it's beautiful exactly.
P No?
M No, I don't really like Gaudi's style, this kind of art ... but, er, it's a special place, for sure. You should see it if you get a chance.
P Right. Have you ever seen the Taj Mahal?
M Well, I've seen it on television.
P OK.
M But no, I haven't been there. What about you?
P No.
M But you're from India, right?
P Yes but India's a big place.
M Hm, OK.
P You know, I've always wanted to go there but when you live in a place ...
M ... you don't always have time to do the tourist things.
P Right. But I've been here, to Angel Falls.
M So you've been to Venezuela?
P Yeah, I had a holiday there.
M Wow.
P Two weeks.
M So what's it like?
P Oh, it's wonderful. The weather was nice and sunny so we had a great view. You know, you can't always see the waterfall.
M Right. So were you on the river or on the mountain ... ?
P Neither. We were in a plane.
M Well, it sounds great – but I think I'd prefer a boat.
P Yeah?
M Yeah, I don't like flying.

3.41
1 Have you been to Güell Park?
  Yes, I have.
2 Have you ever seen the Taj Mahal?
  No, I haven't.
3 I've been to Angel Falls.
4 I've seen it on television.
5 I haven't been there.
6 I've never heard of it.

3.42
1 It's a very unusual place.
2 I've been there lots of times.
3 I've never heard of it.
4 I've seen it on television.
5 What's it like?

3.43
1
KIERAN Graham, hi. A quick question.
GRAHAM Sure. What is it?
K Look, my wife's sister arrived here yesterday ...

G Oh, right. From France?
K Yeah, and, er, we'd like to take her to a nice restaurant tonight.
G OK.
K Er, have you been to that new Italian restaurant, Sicilia?
G No, I haven't, sorry. You could ask Prema.
K OK, I'll ask her. Thanks.

2
KIERAN Hi, Prema?
PREMA Yeah, hi.
K Have you tried Sicilia, the Italian place?
P Yes, we went there two, three weeks ago.
K Right. What was it like?
P Erm ... it was OK but quite expensive.
K Too expensive?
P Hm, yeah. I mean, the food's good, but there are better places.
K Right.
P Why do you ask?
K Oh, my sister-in-law's here and we'd like to take her out tonight.
P Well, let's see ... uh, have you been to Browne's?
K Browne's? The English restaurant?
P No, it's American food. It's really nice.
K OK, I'll think about it. Thanks.

3
KIERAN Monica, can I ask you a question? About restaurants?
MONICA Of course.
K Er, we want to take a guest to dinner tonight. Have you been to Sicilia or Browne's?
M Yes, I have. Both of them.
K Which one should we go to?
M Neither.
K Neither! Why not?
M Sicilia just sells expensive pizzas, and the last time I went to Browne's, the food wasn't very good.
K Oh.
M Take her to Akash.
K Akash? I've never heard of it.
M It's a small restaurant, really nice people, not too expensive, wonderful Indian food. You'll love it. Really.
K OK, I'll try it. Where is it exactly?
M Well, you know the Royal Bank on Chester Street ...

3.44
JESSICA I never really liked shellfish until I went to the north of Spain and some friends took me to a fish restaurant by the sea. They ordered a *zarzuela* which is a huge plate of shellfish. It was a great evening and I was surprised that I really enjoyed the food. After that, I often ate shellfish because it's something people do in Spain on special occasions. It's more than just food. It's like you're celebrating life when you sit down and have *zarzuela* or *paella*.

DAVID I lived in Egypt for a year and I remember walking to work for the first time. It was unbelievably hot and it was only 8 in the morning. As I walked down my street a man came up to me and said "Welcome to Egypt" with a huge smile on his face. I smiled back. It was a lovely moment. As I walked to work four or five more people smiled at me and said "Welcome to Egypt." I couldn't believe how friendly people were to complete strangers, so hospitable. In Britain, most people don't talk to strangers. Yeah, walking around in public in Egypt was completely different.

HYUN Well, I'm Korean but I've always loved Brazilian music. I've got a very big collection of CDs, maybe 250, that I bought in music shops in Seoul and also online. Most of my CDs are samba and Brazilian jazz. I love both kinds of music because they're very lively but also relaxing ... and of course I got interested in Brazil because of the music. I've never been there but I've read a lot about it and I've met a few Brazilians in Seoul. They were really surprised and happy I knew about their music. My dream is to go there and hear the music in its own country one day.

3.46
Starting a conversation:
How are things? | Can you talk now? | Excuse me, have you got a moment? | I haven't seen you for a long time. | Are you doing anything now? | Have you got time for a coffee and a chat?

Finishing a conversation:
I'll talk to you later. | Thanks for your help. | See you at the meeting. | Well, it was good talking to you. | Anyway, I'll text you some time. | Take care.

3.47
RUUD Are you all right?
SALLY No, not really. I've got a headache.
RUUD Oh, I'm sorry to hear that. Maybe you should go home.

3.49
1 whose 2 whisper 3 when
4 whole 5 which 6 why 7 what
8 who 9 white 10 wheel

3.50
SUE Do you think you get enough sleep?
DAN No, not at the moment, because of the baby. I only slept about four hours last night.
S Four hours? Poor you. That's not enough.
D What about you?
S I usually sleep for about nine hours, probably ten at the weekend. And I'm always tired.

D Really? You know, I think that's probably too much sleep. I'm sure it's not good if you get too much.

S Yeah, you may be right. It's nice though!

◆ 3.51

1 Do you think you get enough sleep?

2 Not at the moment, because of the baby.

3 That's not enough.

4 What about you?

5 And I'm always tired.

◆ 3.52

INTERVIEWER Right, in the studio we have Barry Cox, ex-supermarket worker from Liverpool in England, who is now a popular singer in Macau in China. Barry, did you always dream of becoming a singer?

BARRY No, not really. But I knew I wanted to do something different, even when I was a teenager.

I So, what took you to China?

B Well, after I left school at 16 I took up languages. I started Spanish lessons, but then I changed my mind and decided to learn Chinese.

I How did you learn it?

B Well, I walked into my local chip shop and asked the Chinese owners for a meal and language lessons! The owner's nephew wanted English lessons, so we helped each other and became good friends. I met lots of Chinese people in Liverpool through him.

I Did you go to lessons?

B Not exactly! I spent years learning Cantonese with my new friends. I got a job in a Chinese supermarket as well.

I So, when did you decide to become a singer?

B Well, I went to a concert given by Leon Lai, a very popular singer in Hong Kong, and after that I knew exactly what I wanted to do. I entered a singing competition at Chinese New Year. I was awful but people liked me. So after that, I had singing lessons.

I And when did you become successful in China?

B Well, I decided to move abroad, to Hong Kong. After a few years' hard work, I got a job singing Canto-pop, which means popular love songs. I even won a competition. And now I'm singing at a great venue in Macau.

I And you're known as Gok Pak-wing in China?

B That's right. I'm pretty famous!

I So, do you think you've made the right choices in your life?

B Absolutely. I'm having a fantastic time in Macau. When you go back home, you see all of your friends doing

exactly the same as ten years ago. I do things and have done things that most people could only dream of doing.

◆ 3.53

INTERVIEWER And what about the future? What are you going to do next? Are you going to stay in China?

BARRY I'd like to stay in China for a while, yeah. I'm hoping to continue with the singing, yeah. I really love it. But I don't think I want to stay in China for the rest of my life.

I Would you like to move back to Liverpool?

B Well, no, I don't think so. I'm going to stay in China for another few years and see what happens with the singing. I'd like to move to another country one day and learn a new language. Japan could be interesting.

◆ 3.54

1 I'm going to stay in China for another few years.

2 He's hoping to stay in China for another few years.

3 I'd like to stay in China for another few years.

4 Is he going to stay in China next year? Yes, he is. No, he isn't.

5 Are they hoping to move to another country? Yes, they are. No, they aren't.

6 Would you like to move back to Liverpool one day? Yes, I would. No, I wouldn't.

7 What are you going to do this weekend?

◆ 3.55

DAN OK, so what are we going to do about accommodation?

MILLIE Well, let's have a look at the website.

D Hm, this campsite looks nice to me. I think we should stay there.

M Camping! I don't think so! I want to be comfortable.

D Come on, the kids would love it.

M But camping is really uncomfortable. And we need a kitchen, so what about this chalet on the lake?

D Erm … yeah, OK. It looks very nice. Let's try that.

M And what about food?

D Well, we can talk to someone about that when we get there.

M Fine.

D And what are we going to do on Saturday?

M Let's go to the National Park.

D Yeah, we can go hiking or canoeing!

M I suppose so. I'd like to go hiking, I'm not so sure about the canoeing. What about Sunday?

D We could go and watch the bears!

M Er, yes, but it could take a long time before we see one. What about doing the tree-to-tree climbing thing?

D Mmm. I think it's too expensive, it's 25 dollars each. Let's go horse riding.

M Yes, that's a great idea. Everyone will love that. Right, we need to book some of these things then.

◆ 3.56

Introducing / changing topic:
What are we going to do about accommodation?
What are we going to do on Saturday?
Opinions:
I think it's too expensive.
This campsite looks nice to me.
Agreeing / disagreeing:
Yeah, OK.
Fine.
But camping is really uncomfortable.

◆ 3.57

GREG OK, Paula, what things have you tried to learn a language?

PAULA Erm, one thing that really worked for me was, erm, reading magazines and newspapers, erm, especially ads because you have the words and the images together and the sentences are very short so that was very useful.

G Newspapers aren't too difficult?

P Er, well maybe short articles, not the long ones. Erm, and, er, I've tried reading books, longer novels, but that didn't work, at the beginning at least.

G Right.

P What about you?

G Yeah, I've, I've found newspapers too difficult, erm, when I've been learning Japanese but I've, erm, tried reading graded texts and that's helped.

P What do you mean, 'graded texts'?

G Erm, they're designed for people learning the language so they're made simpler.

P OK, like shorter and …

G Yeah.

P OK. Erm, I'm learning German now and what I'd like to try, erm, is to join some sort of, like, speaking … like a discussion group. I've never done that. I think it could be really useful.

G Yeah. I'd like to try a … a language exchange, maybe with a Japanese student.

P And meet and talk.

G Yeah.

◆ 3.58

KHALID I'm going to finish my studies by the end of next year and I will be looking for a job. In the near future, like in the next five or ten years, I hope to start my own business, find someone special and get married, maybe. Erm, one day, I would like to travel around the world.

◆ 3.61

1 walk 2 should 3 comb
4 thumb 5 often 6 designer

Vowels

Short vowels

/ə/	/æ/	/ʊ/	/ɒ/	/ɪ/	/i/	/e/	/ʌ/
teacher ago	married am	book could	on got	in swim	happy easy	wet any	cup under

Long vowels

/ɜː/	/ɑː/	/uː/	/ɔː/	/iː/
her shirt	arm car	blue too	or walk	eat meet

Diphthongs

/eə/	/ɪə/	/ʊə/	/ɔɪ/	/aɪ/	/eɪ/	/əʊ/	/aʊ/
chair where	near we're	tour	boy noisy	nine eye	eight day	go over	out brown

Consonants voiced unvoiced

/b/	/ð/	/v/	/dʒ/	/d/	/z/	/g/	/ʒ/
be bit	mother the	very live	job page	down red	magazine	girl bag	television
/p/	**/θ/**	**/f/**	**/tʃ/**	**/t/**	**/s/**	**/k/**	**/ʃ/**
park shop	think both	face laugh	chips teach	time white	see rice	cold look	shoe fish
/m/	**/n/**	**/ŋ/**	**/l/**	**/r/**	**/w/**	**/j/**	**/h/**
me name	now rain	thing drink	late hello	carry write	we white	you yes	hot hand

Irregular verbs

Infinitive	Past simple	Past participle
All forms are the same		
	cost	
	cut	
	put	
	set	
Past simple and past participle are the same		
bring	brought	
build	built	
buy	bought	
catch	caught	
feel	felt	
find	found	
get	got	
have	had	
hear	heard	
hold	held	
keep	kept	
leave	left	
lose	lost	
make	made	
mean	meant	
meet	met	
pay	paid	
read /riːd/	read /red/	
say	said	
sell	sold	
send	sent	
sit	sat	
spend	spent	
stand	stood	
teach	taught	
tell	told	
think	thought	
understand	understood	
win	won	

Infinitive	Past simple	Past participle
All forms are different		
be	was / were	been
begin	began	begun
break	broke	broken
can	could	been able to
choose	chose	chosen
do	did	done
drink	drank	drunk
drive	drove	driven
eat	ate	eaten
fall	fell	fallen
fly	flew	flown
forget	forgot	forgotten
give	gave	given
go	went	been / gone
know	knew	known
ride	rode	ridden
see	saw	seen
show	showed	shown
sing	sang	sung
speak	spoke	spoken
swim	swam	swum
take	took	taken
wear	wore	worn
write	wrote	written
Infinitive and past participle are the same		
become	became	become
come	came	come
run	ran	run

English Unlimited

A2 Elementary B
Self-study Pack (Workbook)

Maggie Baigent, Chris Cavey & Nick Robinson

CAMBRIDGE
University Press

Contents

8 What's she like?

VOCABULARY
Family

1 Complete what Aziza says about her family using the words in the box.

> aunt ~~brothers~~ children dad grandfather
> grandmother mum nephew niece twins

I have two ¹ *brothers* – George and Hani – and a sister, Camille.
She was born 20 minutes before me, so obviously, we're ² _____ !
My ³ _____ , Elias, is a police officer, and my ⁴ _____ ,
Mariam, looks after the house. My ⁵ _____ and ⁶ _____ ,
Khaled and Amira, live with us, too. George and Hani go to school, and
I'm a student at the university, but Camille is married and has two little
⁷ _____ , so I'm an ⁸ _____ ! My ⁹ _____ , Karim, is
three years old, and my ¹⁰ _____ , Maha, is just four months old.

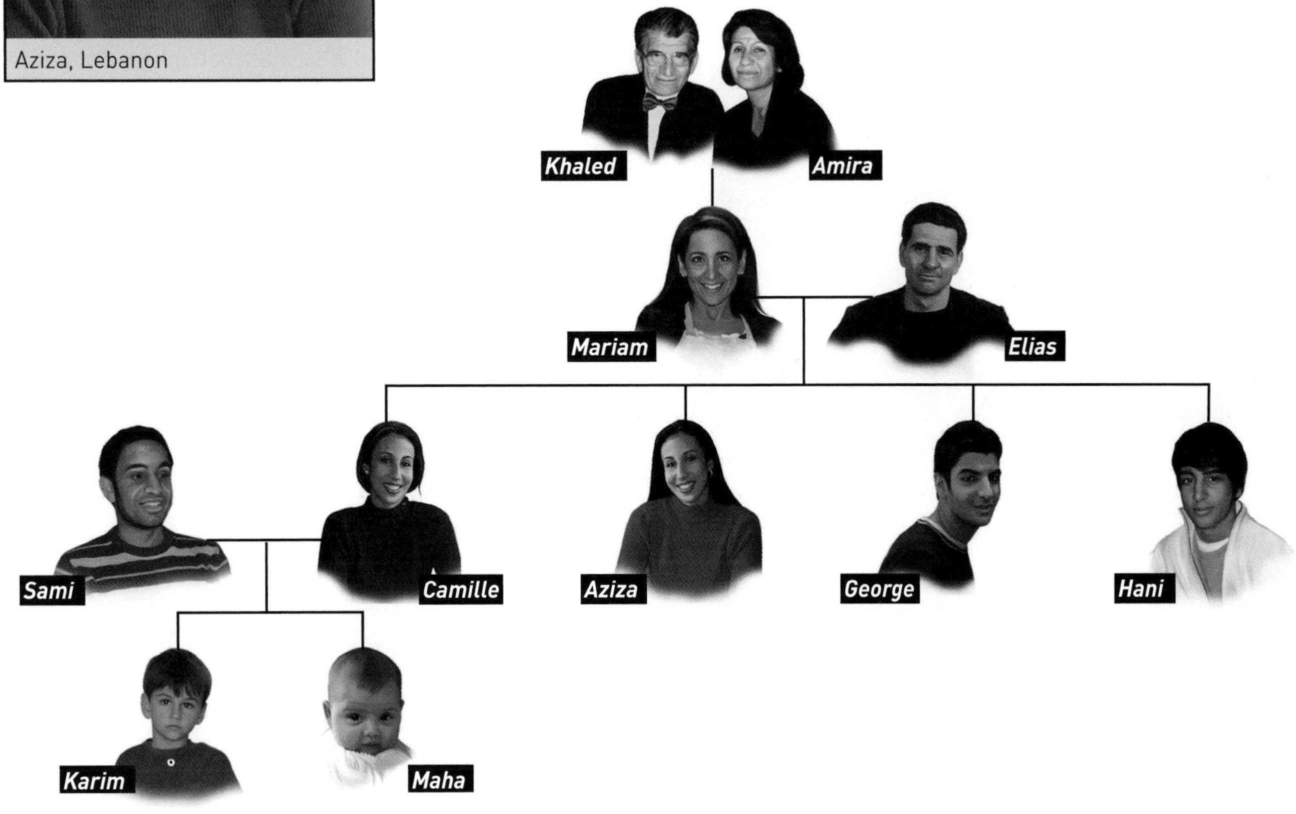

Aziza, Lebanon

Khaled   Amira

Mariam   Elias

Sami   Camille   Aziza   George   Hani

Karim   Maha

VOCABULARY
Personality

2 Circle the correct words to complete what Aziza says about the people in her family.

My sister likes meeting new people – she's very ¹outgoing / hard-
working. Hani makes us all laugh – he's really ²adventurous / funny –
but George is very serious and ³funny / hard-working, like my dad. My
mum is really good at thinking of new ideas – she's a very ⁴creative /
outgoing person. And me? Well, I always like to do new and different
things, so I'm quite ⁵adventurous / funny. And we're all very intelligent,
of course!

Appearance

Over to you

Write a description
of yourself. Write
three sentences.

GRAMMAR

have got

3 Complete the description of Aziza using the words in the box.

| brown | hair | jacket | pale | ~~tall~~ | wearing |

Aziza is ¹____*tall*____ and she's got ²_____ skin.
She's got black ³_____ and ⁴_____ eyes.
She's ⁵_____ trousers. She's not wearing a ⁶_____ .

4 Complete the sentences using the words in the box.

| 've got | Has | ~~'s got~~ | haven't got | hasn't got | Have you got |

1   My mum *'s got* dark hair and brown eyes.
2   I _____ a brother and two sisters.
3   What time is it? _____ a watch?
4   We _____ a car; we use our bikes or public transport.
5   My brother's got a moustache, but he _____ a beard.
6   "_____ your house got a garden?" "No, but there's a big balcony."

5 Complete this paragraph with the correct form of *have got*.

From the early 1900s, most schools in Britain had a uniform to give a sense of school identity. In this picture, the three children are wearing a typical British school uniform from the 1950s. The boy ¹ *'s got* short trousers and long socks. He ²_____ very short hair and a cap on his head. The older girl's uniform is very similar, but she ³_____ trousers – she's wearing a skirt. She ⁴_____ any jewellery. Both of them are wearing shirts and ties, and the school jacket, called a blazer. In many countries around the world, schools ⁵_____ still _____ some kind of uniform for their students today.

Relationships

6 Use the verbs in the box to complete the relationship expressions in bold.

are   get   get   know   like   ~~see~~   spend   talk

1   We don't ____see____ **each other** very often. [NC]
2   We _____ **on** well. ☐
3   We can _____ **about** everything together. ☐
4   We don't _____ **in touch** very often. ☐
5   We _____ **the same things**. ☐
6   We _____ a lot of **time** together. ☐
7   We don't _____ **each other** very well. ☐
8   We _____ very **close**. ☐

Over to you

Think of a person you know. Write three sentences about your relationship.

7 Which sentences in Exercise 6 describe a close relationship? Write C (close) or NC (not close) in each box.

TimeOut

8 Find 15 more words for relatives in the word snake.

1 _aunt_	5 _____	9 _____	13 _____
2 _____	6 _____	10 _____	14 _____
3 _____	7 _____	11 _____	15 _____
4 _____	8 _____	12 _____	16 _____

EXPLORE**Reading**

9   Read the first paragraph of the article. Are the sentences true or false?

1   Nick is a journalist.   TRUE / FALSE
2   He likes formal clothes.   TRUE / FALSE
3   He likes old clothes.   TRUE / FALSE

10 Read what Nick says about his favourite clothes. Match the clothes (1–5) with the places he got them (a–e).

1   scarf   a   in a shop in Australia
2   T-shirt   b   in a shop in Sweden
3   jeans   c   from a friend he worked with
4   jacket   d   from a friend he lived with
5   trainers   e   from his girlfriend's father

Over to you

What's your favourite outfit? Write a description and say where you got the clothes.

11 Read the article again and try to guess the correct options.

1   Katharine Hamnett is a journalist / designer.
2   Glastonbury is a classical / rock and folk music festival.
3   Bondi Beach is famous for surfing / sailing.
4   Stockholm at Christmas is hot / cold.

MY FAVOURITE OUTFIT

Nick Decosemo, 34, musician

Nick was a journalist, but now he has a band and is a DJ. His look is very relaxed. "All my clothes have a story. They are all second-hand." Nick likes the style of Bryan Ferry from Roxy Music and the young Mick Jagger.

JACKET
"When I worked as a journalist at a fashion magazine, my friend Gary, who's a designer, gave me this. It's by Katharine Hamnett, and it's lovely and light."

SCARF
"This belonged to my girlfriend's dad. He was a hippy in the 60s and he wore this to the first Glastonbury music festival in 1970."

T-SHIRT
"I bought this in a surf shop on Bondi Beach, in Sydney. I went to do a concert and I bought some new clothes there."

JEANS
"Last Christmas, I went to Stockholm to do a concert. It was a lovely weekend of hot wine and ice-skating – and I bought these jeans, too."

TRAINERS
"I moved house about three months ago and I found these in the flat. I think they belonged to my old flatmate, Gareth – sorry, Gareth."

1 Before you watch, write down how many people there are in your family.

2 Watch Hitin, Nilgun and Leo talking about their families. Which family is most similar to yours?

Hitin

3 Watch again. Match the speakers with the family trees.

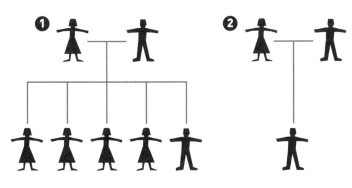

❶ ❷ ❸

_____ _____ _____

Nilgun

4 Watch again and circle the correct answers.

1 Hitin is the oldest / youngest child in his family.
2 His sisters give him / Hitin gives his sisters lots of presents.
3 Nilgun and her twin look / don't look the same.
4 She knows / doesn't know when her twin sister is ill.
5 Leo sees his parents every year / two years.
6 He uses the phone / Internet to talk to his parents.

Leo

5 Can you remember what Hitin, Nilgun and Leo say about their families? Complete the sentences using the words in the box. Watch again to help you.

| call close in touch love lovely make sure mum and dad visit young |

Hitin

1 I have a ___lovely___ family.
2 They _____ me so much.

Nilgun

3 I'm very _____ to my twin sister.
4 We were very naughty when we were _____.
5 I usually _____ her to _____ she's OK.

Leo

6 It is very difficult for me to _____ them.
7 I feel I need to keep _____ with them.
8 It is good for me and also good for my _____.

6 Describe the people in your family. Try to use some expressions from Exercise 5.

GLOSSARY

annual /ˈænjʊəl/ (adjective): every year, or once every year
get told off (verb): If you **get told off**, someone speaks to you in an angry way because you have done something wrong.
gifts (plural noun): A **gift** is a something that you give someone; a present.
identical (adjective): **Identical twins** are formed from the same egg and are exactly the same.
naughty /ˈnɔːti/ (adjective): If a child is **naughty**, he/she does bad things.
youngest (adjective): The last child in a family. The first child is the **oldest**.

Getting around

VOCABULARY
Using transport

1 We asked these people how they get to work. Complete the answers using the phrases in the box.

I get a taxi   I cycle   I drive   I get the bus   ~~I get the train~~   I ride a motorbike

_____*I get the train*_____.
The station is only five minutes from my house.

_____.
It saves money and it helps keep me fit!

I can't drive, but I don't really like public transport, so _____.
It's quite expensive, though.

There's a free car park at work, so _____.

_____.
It's faster than a car and it's easier to park.

Over to you

How often do you do these things? Write a sentence for each one.
get the bus, cycle, get a taxi, get the underground, get the train

I usually walk, but when it's raining, _____.
It stops just outside my office.

VOCABULARY
Getting information

2 Gérard is at the Tourist Information Office. Complete his questions using the words in the box.

best way   do you know   ~~far~~   near here   take

1 Is it _____*far*_____ ?

2 And _____ what time it opens?

3 What's the _____ to get there?

4 Is there a post office _____ ?

5 How long does it _____ to walk?

3 Complete the conversation with the questions from Exercise 2.

GÉRARD Excuse me, ¹ *is there a post office near here?*

ASSISTANT Yes, it's in the square. Opposite the bank.

GÉRARD OK, thanks. ² _____

ASSISTANT You can walk or you can get a bus.

GÉRARD ³ _____

ASSISTANT About a kilometre, more or less.

GÉRARD ⁴ _____

ASSISTANT Not long. About 15 minutes.

GÉRARD Great. ⁵ _____

ASSISTANT Nine thirty.

GRAMMAR
Comparatives
and superlatives

VOCABULARY
Buying a ticket

4 Complete the sentences with the correct form of the adjectives in brackets.

1 What's ___the best___ way to travel in your country? (good)
2 The metro is _____ than the bus in the mornings. (busy)
3 Riding a motorbike is _____ than flying. (dangerous)
4 The underground is _____ way to get around in London. (quick)
5 I think going by train is _____ than going
  by car. (interesting)
6 What's _____ way to get to the airport? (easy)

5 Think of two towns or cities you know well. Write five more comparative sentences about them. Use some of the adjectives in the box.

| beautiful   busy   clean   expensive   interesting |

1 *I think (San Francisco) is more beautiful than (New York).* _____
2 _____
3 _____
4 _____
5 _____
6 _____

6 Complete the train ticket using the words in the box.

Departure
Direct
From
Price
~~return~~

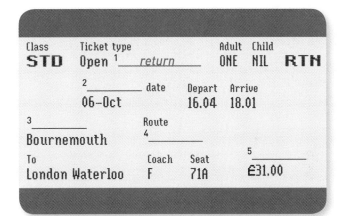

Class	Ticket type		Adult	Child	
STD	Open ¹___return___		**ONE**	**NIL**	**RTN**

² _____ date   Depart Arrive
06-Oct   16.04   18.01

³ _____   Route
Bournemouth   ⁴ _____

To   Coach Seat   ⁵ _____
London Waterloo   F   71A   £31.00

7 Write the customer's questions in the correct order.

CUSTOMER Excuse me, get / how / it / London / take / long / to / to / does / ?
1 _____

ASSISTANT About two hours.

CUSTOMER And open / does / how / an / please / return / cost, / much / ?
2 _____

ASSISTANT It's £31.00.

CUSTOMER OK, and is / direct / it / ?
3 _____

ASSISTANT Yes, you don't need to change.

CUSTOMER What / leave / does / the / train / time / next / ?
4 _____

ASSISTANT At 16.04. In about half an hour.

MYEnglish

8 Read the text. Are the sentences true or false?

"I work for an American bank in Tokyo, so I speak English every day. I studied English for eight years at school and college, and I use it every day, so my English is OK – but I still find some things difficult. English pronunciation is difficult for me – and for lots of Japanese people. The sound 'th' is hard – we don't have this sound in Japanese. And I find it hard to say 'l' and 'r', too. I think people at the bank understand me, though. When I started learning English, I made mistakes with nouns, adjectives and adverbs – often it's the same word in Japanese – so I'd say 'Tokyo is a very safety city' instead of 'Tokyo is a very safe city'. I don't often make that kind of mistake now, though.

One more thing – English is everywhere in Japan! I read advertisements and everything I see in English. It helps me remember words."

Yuko, Japan

1 Yuko is a college student.   TRUE / FALSE
2 English pronunciation is difficult for Yuko.   TRUE / FALSE
3 Yuko sees lots of English in Japan.   TRUE / FALSE

Your English

9 Yuko finds some sounds difficult to pronounce in English. Here are some problem words for her.
What are the problem sounds in English for you? Add your own sounds and words to the list.

/r/	right, read
/l/	light, lead

10 Sometimes adjectives, nouns and adverbs in English are the same word in other languages. Circle the correct word in each sentence.

1 My grandfather is a very happy / happiness person.
2 You're walking very slow / slowly. Come on, hurry up!
3 Riding a motorbike is quite danger / dangerous.
4 The metro is very busy / business in the morning.
5 Taxis are quite expensive / expense.

11 Yuko says that she sees lots of things in English in Japan. Do you see advertisements and other things in English where you live? Make a list.

EXPLORE Writing

12   Look at the 'On foot' section of the party invitation. Circle the correct answers and
      write them in the gaps.

	a		b		c	
1	a	Out of	b	From	c	Across
2	a	out of	b	down	c	up
3	a	to	b	from	c	across
4	a	down	b	into	c	from
5	a	through	b	down	c	up
6	a	out of	b	up	c	into

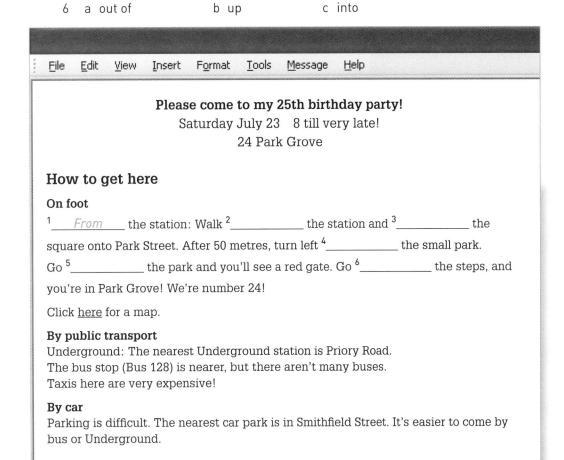

File   Edit   View   Insert   Format   Tools   Message   Help

Please come to my 25th birthday party!
Saturday July 23   8 till very late!
24 Park Grove

How to get here

On foot

¹ ___From___ the station: Walk ² _____ the station and ³ _____ the
square onto Park Street. After 50 metres, turn left ⁴ _____ the small park.
Go ⁵ _____ the park and you'll see a red gate. Go ⁶ _____ the steps, and
you're in Park Grove! We're number 24!

Click here for a map.

By public transport
Underground: The nearest Underground station is Priory Road.
The bus stop (Bus 128) is nearer, but there aren't many buses.
Taxis here are very expensive!

By car
Parking is difficult. The nearest car park is in Smithfield Street. It's easier to come by
bus or Underground.

13   Read the invitation again. Which map is correct?

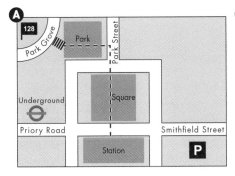
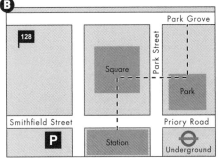
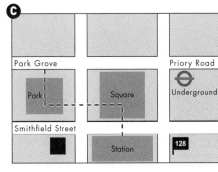

14   Look at the 'By public transport' and 'By car' sections and find:

      1   two comparatives
      2   two superlatives

15   Imagine you are planning a party at your home. Write notes for your invitation
      telling people how to get there – on foot and by public transport. Try to use at least
      one superlative and one comparative.

1 You are going to watch Claire talking about a long trip to Australia. Before you watch, look at this list. Which of these things do you think she talks about?

learning English ☑   snakes ☐
dolphins ☐   spiders ☐
kangaroos ☐   Sydney ☐
pizza ☐   trucks ☐

2 Watch parts 1 and 2 of the video. Tick (✓) the things from Exercise 1 that Claire mentions.

3 Watch part 1 of the video again (00:10–01:15) and (circle) the correct answers.

Claire Bauden was ¹18 / 19 and was a student at university in ²Australia / France. She decided to go to Perth and she stayed there for two ³years / months. At first, she ⁴could understand everything / couldn't understand anything. After six ⁵weeks / months, she felt more comfortable, so she decided to travel around Australia with a friend.

4 Watch part 2 of the video again (01:18–02:45). Claire says they decided to 'hitchhike'. Which picture shows how Claire travelled round Australia?

1    **2**    **3**

5 Watch part 2 again. Put the pictures in the right order.

 ☐    ☐    ☐    ☐    1

6 Claire uses some Australian words. What do you think they mean? Match the words (1–3) with the definitions (a–c).

1 g'day   a a large, empty area of land
2 the bush   b a lorry driver
3 a truckie   c hello

7 Claire and her friend hitchhiked across Australia. Would you ever hitchhike like this? Explain why / why not.

GLOSSARY

accent (noun): Your **accent** is the way you pronounce words. Some people have strong accents that are difficult to understand.
bilingual (adjective): If you are **bilingual**, you can speak two languages fluently.
hitchhike (verb): to travel by getting free rides in other people's cars and lorries
trailer (noun): something pulled behind a car or lorry
satellite phone (noun): a mobile phone that works in remote areas, for example in the desert

10 Getting together

1 (Circle) the correct words or phrases to complete the descriptions.

1 an animated film: a film with human actors / cartoons or models
2 a comedy: a funny / sad film that makes you laugh / cry
3 a horror film: a funny / scary film about nice / horrible things
4 a drama: a funny / serious film with an interesting story
5 a romantic film: a film about love / war
6 an action film: a boring / an exciting film where a lot / not a lot of things happen
7 a documentary: a film about real / imaginary people or things
8 a science-fiction film: a film set in the past / future or another part of the universe

2 Write the words in the correct order to complete the conversation.

ANNA   If you're not doing anything this evening, ¹ you / come / like / would / to
would you like to come over to my house? ² could / We / get
_____ a pizza and watch a film.

SONIA   ³ good / sounds / That _____ .

ANNA   OK. I've got an old Hitchcock film we could watch.

SONIA   Hmm. ⁴ not / I'm / sure _____ . I don't usually like thrillers.
⁵ we / DVD / Why / rent / don't / a _____ ?

ANNA   ⁶ with / me / Fine _____ .

3 Complete the sentences using the verbs in the box in the present progressive.

arrive   come   come back   fly   go   ~~stay~~   wait   not work

1 Dr Sharma's here for a conference. He _'s staying_ in a hotel in the centre of town.
2 They _____ to my house this evening to watch a film.
3 I _____ to Qatar tomorrow on the midday flight.
4 We _____ camping in Greece this summer.
5 The train _____ at the station.
6 I _____ from my trip on Sunday night.
7 Where are you? We _____ for you!
8 She's got baby twins, so she _____ at the moment.

4 Which sentences in Exercise 3 are about now and which are about future arrangements? Write N (now) or F (future) in the boxes.

5 Complete the time expressions in bold with *in*, *on* or *at* if necessary. Some expressions don't need a preposition.

1 They're leaving __on__ **Saturday morning**.

2 We're going to Morocco _____ **next month**.

3 I'm going to the dentist's _____ **this afternoon**.

4 My grandfather's having his 90th birthday party _____ **14th May**!

5 We're leaving _____ **tonight**.

6 They're having another meeting _____ **tomorrow**.

7 Their train's arriving _____ **6.15**.

8 I'm going on holiday _____ **August**.

6 Look at Liz's desk. Tick (✓) the true sentences and correct the false ones.

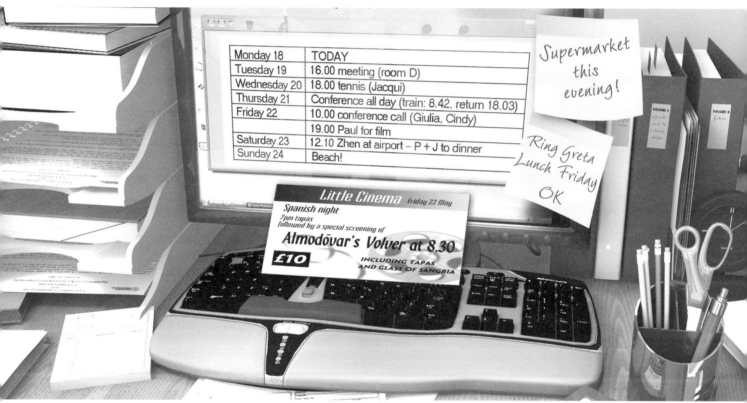

Monday 18	TODAY
Tuesday 19	16.00 meeting (room D)
Wednesday 20	18.00 tennis (Jacqui)
Thursday 21	Conference all day (train: 8.42, return 18.03)
Friday 22	10.00 conference call (Giulia, Cindy)
	19.00 Paul for film
Saturday 23	12.10 Zhen at airport – P + J to dinner
Sunday 24	Beach!

Supermarket this evening!

Ring Greta Lunch Friday OK

Little Cinema *friday 22 May*
Spanish night
7pm tapas
followed by a special screening of
Almodóvar's Volver at 8.30
£10 INCLUDING TAPAS AND GLASS OF SANGRIA

Liz, Scotland

Over to you

Look at your diary and write three sentences about your arrangements.

1 She's playing tennis on Wednesday morning.
She's playing tennis on Wednesday evening / at 6 pm on Wednesday.

2 She's going shopping this evening.
_____

3 She's not working in the office on Thursday.
_____

4 She's speaking to Giulia on Friday afternoon.
_____

5 She's seeing friends on Saturday evening.
_____

6 She's having a meeting tomorrow afternoon.
_____

7 She's staying at home on Friday evening.
_____

8 She's meeting Zhen at the airport on Sunday.
_____

VOCABULARY

Talking about films 2

7 Complete the film review using the words and phrases in the box.

> character   directed by   ~~drama~~   funny   it's about   set in   stars

Volver

Volver (2006) is a ¹ _____drama_____ written and ² _____ Pedro Almodóvar. It is ³ _____ a village in Spain, and ⁴ _____ a family – two sisters, their aunt and the teenage daughter of one of the sisters. Another ⁵ _____ is the sisters' dead mother, who comes back to help them in a difficult time; *volver* means 'to return' in Spanish. It ⁶ _____ Penélope Cruz, but the cast really work as a team; in fact, six actresses shared the Best Actress award at the Cannes Film Festival. *Volver* is a warm, ⁷ _____ film about the relationship between women.

TimeOut

8 How much do you know about the cinema? Do the quiz!

1 abc

2 What nationality is the actor Gael García Bernal?
  a Mexican   **b** Argentinian   **c** Spanish

3 Where does the director Ang Lee come from?
  a The United States   **b** Taiwan   **c** Korea

4 Which city is the Bollywood film industry based in?
  a Delhi   **b** Kolkata   **c** Mumbai

5 Which rock band made the film *Tommy*?
  a Pink Floyd   **b** The Who   **c** Rolling Stones

6 Which country makes the most films in Arabic?
  a Egypt   **b** Tunisia   **c** Syria

7 Which film is NOT Chinese?
  a *Red Sorghum*   **b** *Farewell My Concubine*   **c** *Spirited Away*

8 Who is the voice of Donkey in the *Shrek* films?
  a Mike Myers   **b** Antonio Banderas   **c** Eddie Murphy

Answers
1 c   2 a   3 b   4 c ('The old name of the city was Bombay.)   5 b   6 a
7 c (It's Japanese.)   8 c

EXPLORE Reading

9 Look at the page from the *Summer in the City* programme. Tick (✓) the kinds of events that are featured.

Theatre ✓ Jazz ☐
Classical music ☐ Folk music ☐
Film ☐ Walks ☐
Dance ☐ Rock music ☐
Children's events ☐ Talks ☐

10 Are these sentences true or false?

1 All the music events are free. TRUE / FALSE
2 You don't have to pay to see the film. TRUE / FALSE
3 The most expensive event is a live show. TRUE / FALSE
4 Adults cannot sleep in the park after *Clowns*. TRUE / FALSE

11 Which event do you choose if ...

1 you want to dance until late at night?
2 you are interested in history?
3 you want to take your eight-year-old daughter out?
4 you want to have a drink and listen to some relaxing music?

Summer in the City
Saturday 12 July

CINEMA UNDER THE STARS
Piazza Grande 22.00

The Man Without a Past
by Aki Kaurismaki (Finland, 2003)

Free

SPECIAL EVENT
Arena Sport 21.30

Fura dels Baus
Spectacular performance by the celebrated Catalan theatre company in their new all-women production, *Imperium*

€30
Information and tickets from Tourist Information Office, Piazza Grande
Mon–Sat 14.00–19.00

KIDS' SUMMER
Guasto Gardens 20.00

Clowns

A fun show for the under-12s, inspired by Fellini's clowns. After the show, kids and their families are invited to sleep under the stars in the park!

Free, but book in advance
339 3450228

SCANDELLARA FESTIVAL
Scandellara Park 21.00–02.00

Jurassic Rock in concert 22.00
Plus DJ

Free

CITY WALKS
Starting from Piazza Piccola 21.00

Secrets of the Middle Ages: the city in the 13th and 14th century
The walk lasts approximately two hours.

€8 Book in advance 348 4499321

OPEN-AIR JAZZ
Via del Porto 21.30

Music from the Max Aurora trio

Entrance and first drink €5

CLASSICAL COURTYARD
De Pisis Gallery main courtyard 21.30

Music by Schubert, Beethoven and Dvorak
Donatella Virzi, piano

Free

1   Before you watch, look at this list of types of film and tick (✓) the ones you like.

		Exercise 1	Exercise 2
1	comedies	☐	A
2	Indian cinema	☐	☐
3	romantic comedies	☐	☐
4	serious documentaries	☐	☐
5	romantic love stories	☐	☐

2   Watch Amanda and Hitin talking about films. Who talks about the types of films in Exercise 1? Write A (Amanda) or H (Hitin).

Amanda

Hitin

3   Watch Amanda again (00:10–00:39) and (circle) the correct answers.

1   Why can Amanda go to the cinema without paying?
    a) She works there.   b) Her husband works there.
2   Why did they go to see films more often in the past?
    a) Because now they need a babysitter for their son.
    b) Because their son doesn't like films.
3   What kind of films do Amanda and her husband go to see?
    a) science-fiction films   b) comedies and more serious films

4   Complete the information about Indian films using the words in the box. Watch Hitin again (00:40–01:54) to help you.

characters family friends fun happy love story songs

Indian films have 'larger than life' ¹ _characters_ , and they are really ² _____ .

They are usually a romantic ³ _____ , and most films have a ⁴ _____

ending. They are different from American movies because they have a lot of

⁵ _____ . Indian films reflect Indian culture and are usually about

⁶ _____ and ⁷ _____ .

5   Match the beginnings and endings of the sentences to make sentences that Amanda and Hitin say. Watch again to check.

1   I like ...   a   when I was a small baby.
2   We also see ...   b   Indian cinema.
3   I'm a huge fan of ...   c   some serious documentaries.
4   My love for Indian cinema began ... d   romantic comedy.

6   Describe the type of films people in your country like.

GLOSSARY

bonding (noun): a close feeling or relationship between people
ending (noun): the end; the way a story or film finishes
for free (expression): If you can do something **for free**, you don't pay any money.
larger than life (adjective phrase): A person who is **larger than life** seems very interesting or different from normal people.
look after (verb): If you **look after** children, you care for them and keep them safe.
projectionist (noun): A **projectionist** is the person who operates the equipment (the **projector**) to show the film in a cinema.

Journeys

11

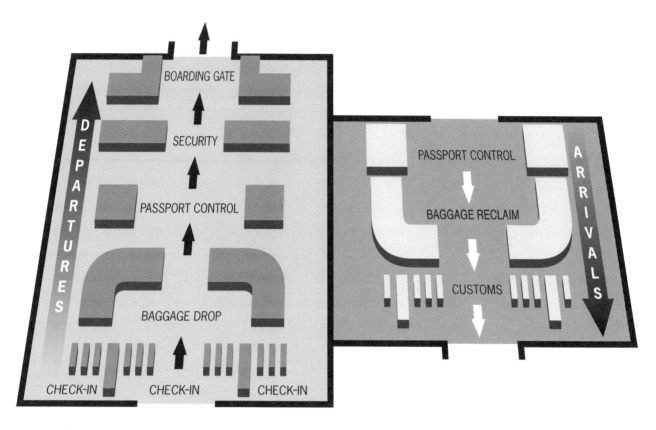

BOARDING GATE

SECURITY

PASSPORT CONTROL

DEPARTURES

BAGGAGE DROP

CHECK-IN   CHECK-IN   CHECK-IN

PASSPORT CONTROL

BAGGAGE RECLAIM

CUSTOMS

ARRIVALS

VOCABULARY

Airports

1 Find places in the airport where you do these things.

When you start your journey, ...

1 you and your bags are checked here for dangerous things.   _security_

2 you go here to show your ticket or boarding pass before you fly.   _____

3 your plane leaves from here.   _____

4 you leave your big bags here.   _____

When you arrive at your destination, ...

5 your bags arrive here.   _____

6 you have to go through here before you leave the airport.   _____

7 you show your passport here.   _____

2 Complete the airport sentences using the words in the box.

anything	bag	belt	gate	keys	laptop	~~luggage~~	pack	passport

1 Do you have any hand _luggage_ ?   ☐ C

2 Are you wearing a _____ ?   ☐

3 Can I see your _____ and ticket, please?   ☐

4 Did you _____ your bag yourself?   ☐

5 Do you have a _____ in your bag?   ☐

6 Boarding is at 10.25 from _____ 12.   ☐

7 Do you have any _____ in your bag?   ☐

8 Would you open your _____ , please?   ☐

9 Are you carrying _____ for anyone else?   ☐

3 Where do you hear the sentences in Exercise 2? Write C (check-in) or S (security).

Articles

Montse, Spain

4 Number the sentences 1–5 to tell Montse's story.

a ☐ At the end of my holiday, I bought a special bag and put the cat in it.
b ☐ I took it to my holiday apartment and gave it food every day.
c ☐ In the end, I paid a lot of money to bring the cat into the country; I think I have the most expensive cat in the world!
d ☐1 I love cats, and when I was on holiday in Greece, I found a beautiful little cat.
e ☐ I had no problems when I left Greece, but when I arrived at the airport in my country, the Customs officials took the cat from me.

5 Match the phrases from the story (1–10) with the rules (a–f).

1 at **the** end of my holiday
2 I bought **a** special bag
3 put **the** cat in it
4 gave it food
5 **the** most expensive cat
6 in **the** world
7 I love cats
8 **a** beautiful little cat
9 at **the** airport
10 took **the** cat from me

a Use *a/an* to talk about a person or thing for the first time.   ☐2 ☐
b Use *the* when the reader or listener knows which thing.   ☐ ☐
c Use – (no article) to talk about things in general.   ☐ ☐
d Use *the* with some time expressions.   ☐
e Use *the* with some place expressions.   ☐ ☐
f Use *the* with some adjectives.   ☐

VOCABULARY

Storytelling expressions

Elke, Germany

6 Complete Elke's travel story using the expressions in the box.

a few years ago	and then	at the time	I was with	In the end
in the middle of	It was quite frightening	the south of		

Well, this was ¹ _a few years ago_ in Africa. I was in Tanzania ² _____ . I was in the Selous Park in ³ _____ the country, on a safari trip. ⁴ _____ my husband, the driver of the car and another guide. We crossed a dry river, ⁵ _____ the driver stopped the car because there was a huge mother elephant ⁶ _____ the road, about ten metres in front of us. She was dangerous because her baby was near; we couldn't go back and we couldn't continue driving. ⁷ _____ , the elephant walked away to her baby. ⁸ _____ , but I got some great photos!

VOCABULARY

Talking about
a journey

Over to you

Talk about a
journey you went
on. Use some
expressions from
Exercise 7.

7 Cross out the words or expressions that are *not* correct.

1 We booked / went / found seats on a flight to New York.
2 We drove / went / waited to the airport.
3 We showed our passport / shopping / ticket at check-in.
4 The flight was on time / delayed / checked.
5 We cancelled / caught / missed our connection in Amsterdam.
6 We spent / waited / wanted six hours in the airport.
7 The airport was very comfortable / uncomfortable / delayed.
8 The flight left / started / took off at 11.30 at night.
9 The plane checked / landed / arrived in New York the next afternoon.
10 We stayed / were / delayed in a three-star hotel on Broadway.

MYEnglish

8 Read what Nadya says, and choose the correct way to
complete the sentences.

1 Nadya speaks good / a little English.
2 She likes reading / listening to English.

> " I really like travelling, and now I can speak a little bit of English, I see and hear
> it everywhere, even in my own country. I like to practise reading signs and
> advertisements, because my language uses a different alphabet, but when
> people speak to me, I get very nervous and I don't always understand. I try to
> imagine the questions that people can ask me and I practise conversations with
> myself. And sometimes I ask people for information just to practise! I smile and
> ask politely, so I think it's OK. "

Nadya, Ukraine

9 Which communication strategies does Nadya use?

1 She reads words on signs. ✓
2 She practises pronouncing words she sees. ☐
3 She learns and practises key words before she travels. ☐
4 She imagines the questions people will ask. ☐
5 She practises conversations with herself. ☐
6 She practises expressions to check she understands. ☐
7 She practises expressions to ask people to repeat. ☐
8 She tries asking people questions. ☐

Your English

10 Tick (✓) the strategies you use. Write ! for strategies you would
like to try.

11 Do you remember these questions you can use to ask people for
help when you don't understand?
Complete them using the words in the box.

how much   say   slow down   spell   understand   which

1 Sorry, could you _____say_____ that again, please?
2 I'm sorry, I don't _____.
3 Could you _____ the name for me, please?
4 Sorry, _____ did you say? €3.50?
5 Sorry, can you _____ a bit?
6 Sorry, _____ platform?

EXPLORE Writing

12 Read the letter and (circle) the correct words.

1 Ms Bruckner travelled by plane / (ferry).
2 She is writing to the travel company / a friend.
3 She went to Italy / Greece.
4 The boat was delayed / cancelled.
5 She wants to book another journey / an apology and some money.

24 September

Dear Sir or Madam

1 I am writing <u>to complain</u> about a journey with your company on 4 August from Brindisi, Italy, to Patras, Greece.

2 Our ferry <u>was delayed</u> by ten hours, but your <u>staff</u> didn't give us any information, and there was no shop or café to buy any food or drinks. When we got on the boat, it was dirty and uncomfortable. There were no <u>free seats</u>, and my three children and I slept on the floor in the bar.

3 I am not <u>satisfied</u> with your service and I hope <u>to receive</u> an apology and <u>some compensation</u> for our uncomfortable journey. I look forward to your reply.

Yours faithfully

Clara Bruckner

Clara Bruckner

13 How is the letter organised? Which paragraph (1, 2 or 3) ...

a asks for a reply? ☐
b says why Clara is writing? ☐
c gives information about the problem? ☐

14 Match the <u>underlined</u> words and expressions in the letter with the definitions.

1 the people who work for a company *staff*
2 places to sit _____
3 to say I am not happy _____
4 to get _____
5 was late _____
6 happy _____
7 some money _____

15 Find expressions in the letter that are used to ...

1 start the letter _____
2 say why you are writing _____
3 say you want the person to write back to you _____
4 end the letter _____

flight 15 hours delayed
no information
no food, expensive drinks
no seats in airport, sat on floor
old, dirty plane

16 You had a very bad flight with BestOne airlines. Use the notes on the left to write a letter to complain.

1   Before you watch, look at these countries. Which ones, if any, have you visited?

    Croatia   Italy   Japan   Mexico   Poland   the USA

2   Watch Justyna and Luis talking about trips. Which two countries did they visit?

Justyna

Luis

_____   _____

3   Watch again and (circle) the correct answers.

Justyna

1   Justyna went to Croatia on holiday / (for work).
2   Justyna thought Croat and Polish were similar / very different.
3   'False friends' are words that sound the same but have a different meaning / spelling.
4   Justyna wanted to ask how long it would take to iron a shirt / some trousers.
5   *Godzina* means 'hour' in Polish and 'week' / 'year' in Croat.

Luis

6   Luis flew over the Grand Canyon in a helicopter / plane.
7   He sat in the back / front seat.
8   The floor was made of metal / glass.
9   They flew for an hour / a couple of hours.

4   Complete the sentences using the adjectives in the box. Watch again to check.

> amazing   confident   excited   offended

1   I went to a conference in Croatia, and I was very _____ – I was quite _____.

2   I wanted to ask the lady how long it would take to iron my trousers, and she got quite _____.

3   It was an _____ experience that I will never forget.

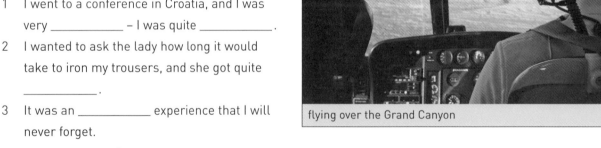
flying over the Grand Canyon

5   Justyna talks about 'false friends' – words that sound similar to a word in your language but have a different meaning. What 'false friends' can you think of?

6   Describe a trip you have taken. Where did you go? What did you do? What did you like / not like?

GLOSSARY

conference (noun): a big meeting with talks on a particular subject
canyon (noun): a big valley with steep sides, like the Grand Canyon in Arizona, USA
cliff (noun): a high wall of rock, often (but not always) near the sea
iron (verb): to make clothes flat and smooth
offended (adjective): If you are **offended**, your feelings are hurt.

12 Are you OK?

VOCABULARY

The body and health

1 Complete the names of the parts of the body.

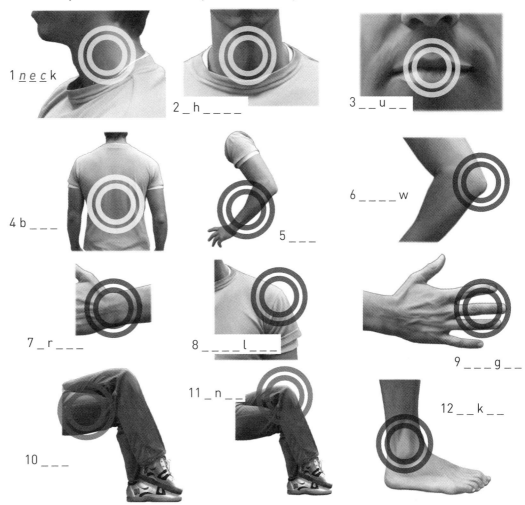

1 n e c k

2 _ h _ _ _ _

3 _ _ u _ _

4 b _ _ _

5 _ _ _

6 _ _ _ _ w

7 _ r _ _ _

8 _ _ _ _ l _ _ _

9 _ _ _ g _ _

10 _ _ _

11 _ n _ _

12 _ _ k _ _

2 Use the words and expressions in the box to complete the medicine instructions.

> allergic to   children under 12   every four to six hours   Keep away from
> sore throat   ~~symptoms~~   WARNING!

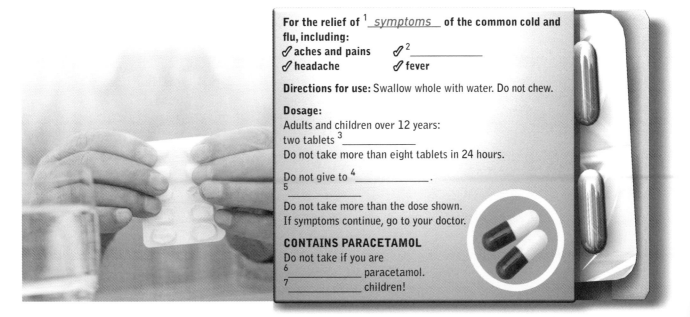

For the relief of [1] _symptoms_ **of the common cold and flu, including:**
☑ aches and pains   ☑ [2]_____
☑ headache   ☑ fever

Directions for use: Swallow whole with water. Do not chew.

Dosage:
Adults and children over 12 years:
two tablets [3]_____
Do not take more than eight tablets in 24 hours.

Do not give to [4]_____.
[5]
_____
Do not take more than the dose shown.
If symptoms continue, go to your doctor.

CONTAINS PARACETAMOL
Do not take if you are
[6]_____ paracetamol.
[7]_____ children!

3 Look at Gabor and Lydia's problems. Circle the correct words in the advice below. Then mark each piece of advice G (Gabor) or L (Lydia).

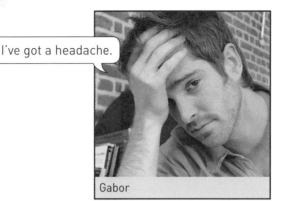

I've got a headache.

Gabor

I want to stay healthy at work.

Lydia

1 *Don't sit* / *Sit* near the air-conditioner. It's bad for your eyes and skin.

L

2 You *should* / *shouldn't* see a doctor – it might be something serious.

☐

3 You *should* / *shouldn't* go out for a walk – it's not good to be inside all day.

☐

4 *Get* / *Don't get* some plants – they'll make your desk look nicer.

☐

5 You *should* / *shouldn't* put salt water in your ears. It can help the pain stop. But don't use really hot water!

☐

6 *Take* / *Don't take* a paracetamol and lie down for half an hour.

☐

7 You *should* / *shouldn't* keep the window closed – you need fresh air!

☐

8 *Listen* / *Don't listen* to loud music!

☐

4 Françoise wants to keep fit. Write three pieces of advice for her.

5 Read the advice on how to stay healthy at work. Match the beginnings (1–6) with the endings (a–f).

1 ☐ f ☐ You should sit near a window if …
2 ☐ If you want to improve the appearance of your office, …
3 ☐ You should change the colour of your office walls if …
4 ☐ You should open a window in your office …
5 ☐ If you want to keep fit, …
6 ☐ If you don't want to get back pain, …

a … get some plants.
b … if possible.
c … make sure you have the right chair.
d … you feel bored.
e … use the stairs, not the lift.
f … you can.

Collocations

6 Complete the diagrams using the words in the box.

a meeting   a party   a train   fun   lunch   money   tablets   ~~time~~

_____   _____

have

_____   _____

spend

time

_____

take

_____   _____

7 Complete the sentences with collocations from Exercise 6.

1 Do you want to ___*have*___ ___*lunch*___ next week? There's a new café on the high street.
2 It'll be quicker to _____ _____ – the traffic is always bad at this time of day.
3 Did you _____ _____ at Isabel's party?
4 We should _____ _____ in the office next week. We need to discuss this face to face.
5 I know I should _____ more _____ with my family, but I'm too busy at work!

TimeOut

8 Find 15 more parts of the body.

L	Q	Z	E	W	Y	W	T	U	S	P	I	G	S	M
Y	K	Y	U	B	F	U	H	R	S	N	A	D	Q	D
E	T	I	V	O	Z	T	R	U	M	K	Z	L	T	Q
N	E	C	K	H	N	O	O	Z	F	C	I	R	L	N
C	S	V	I	E	Q	E	A	E	U	T	L	N	J	U
C	T	M	Y	A	B	G	T	K	U	S	A	B	K	T
T	O	U	G	D	Y	Z	Y	Z	N	E	E	A	O	F
F	M	S	P	O	V	P	Q	N	I	E	W	C	D	A
D	A	C	B	U	O	K	S	X	M	S	E	K	K	C
T	C	L	H	E	S	Y	R	F	I	N	G	E	R	E
G	H	E	E	A	N	K	L	E	W	J	R	A	P	F
F	U	F	H	J	L	S	M	V	X	H	E	Z	S	N
G	L	B	N	M	U	F	O	O	T	V	Y	K	V	X
Y	J	E	M	O	U	T	H	I	L	M	L	C	L	O
I	Q	M	G	P	C	H	S	H	O	U	L	D	E	R

EXPLORE Reading

9   Read the advice about flying. Put these headings (1–3) in the correct places (A–C).

1   Before you fly
2   Flying with children
3   In the plane

✈ STAY HEALTHY WHEN YOU FLY

A _____

1   Take lots of water to the airport with you. Drink it regularly.
2   Make sure you have lots of time to get to the airport. Check that the roads are clear or the trains are on time.
3   Before you get on your flight, go for a quick walk in the airport to get some exercise.
4   _____

B _____

5   Don't drink coffee or alcohol.
6   Get up and have a walk for five or ten minutes every hour. Don't just sit in your seat.
7   Keep any medicine you need in your hand luggage.
8   _____

C _____

9   Call the airline before you travel. Ask if they do anything special for children.
10 Give yourself lots and lots of time to do anything! Children don't always move quickly.
11 Bring something for children to do in the airport and on the plane.
12 _____

10 Write the three extra pieces of advice in the correct sections of the leaflet.

a   Read a book or do a puzzle before you get on the flight. It will help you stop feeling nervous.
b   Bring some snacks – children might not like the food on the plane.
c   Don't sit with your legs crossed. Move your legs to get some exercise in your seat.

11 Match the pictures (a–f) with the correct piece of advice in the leaflet.

12 Look at the pictures in Exercise 11 and decide if they are things you *should* or *shouldn't* do according to the leaflet. Put a tick (✓) beside the things you *should* do and put a cross (✗) beside the things you *shouldn't* do.

1   Before you watch, look at the photos. Which do you think is most important for a healthy lifestyle?

exercise ☐

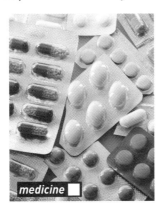

medicine ☐

sleep ☐

diet ☐

2   Watch Lona talking about a healthy lifestyle. Number the photos in Exercise 1 in the order she talks about them.

3   Watch again and (circle) the correct answers.

    1   Lona likes to sleep (eight) / ten hours a day.
    2   She thinks going to the gym is boring / fun.
    3   She goes to dance classes once / a couple of times a week.
    4   She prefers to eat white / brown rice and wholemeal / white bread.
    5   She buys organic food / goes to a restaurant when she has some money.
    6   Her family uses Ayurvedic / Western medicine at home.

4   Match the phrases to make sentences. Watch again to check.

    1   She sleeps   a   honey   i   because it gives energy.
    2   She drinks   b   for eight hours   ii   when she isn't feeling well.
    3   She takes   c   turmeric in warm milk   iii   to feel good.

5   Match the beginnings and endings of the sentences. Watch again to check.

    1   It's really important to ...   a   ... exercise.
    2   Another thing that's really important is ...   b   ... I like to take.
    3   I hate activities like ...   c   ... respect one's pattern of sleeping.
    4   I tend to eat ...   d   ... going to the gym.
    5   There are some other things that ...   e   ... things like brown rice.

6   Describe your lifestyle. Is it like Lona's? Try to use expressions from Exercise 5.

GLOSSARY

Ayurvedic medicine (noun): traditional Indian medicine
components (plural noun): the different parts of something
side effect (noun): A **side effect** of a medicine is an extra, negative effect.
turmeric (noun): a yellow spice
wholemeal (adjective): **Wholemeal** bread is made from brown flour, not white, so it's more natural.

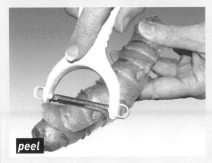

peel

grate

strain

Experiences

GRAMMAR

Present perfect

1 Match the sentence beginnings (1–12) with the correct endings (a–l). There may be more than one possible answer.

1	I've never met	a	a book in English.
2	I've never used	b	a cigarette.
3	I've never smoked	c	a telephone meeting.
4	I've never eaten	d	a member of a gym.
5	I've never been	e	watching sport on TV.
6	I've never played	f	a famous person.
7	I've never worked	g	a horror film.
8	I've never read	h	to be rich.
9	I've never liked	i	an MP3 player.
10	I've never had	j	golf.
11	I've never seen	k	after midnight.
12	I've never wanted	l	Japanese food.

2 Complete the table. Use the sentences in Exercise 1 to help you.

	Verb	Past participle
Regular verbs (–ed)	*use*	*used*
	_____	_____
	_____	_____
	_____	_____
	_____	_____
	_____	_____
Irregular	meet	_____
	eat	_____
	be	_____
	read	_____
	have	_____
	see	_____

Over to you

Write three things you've never done and three things you've always wanted to do. Use verbs from the table in Exercise 2.

VOCABULARY

Sights

3 Label the postcards using the words in the box.

castle   city walls   fountain   museum   palace
ruins   sculpture   statue   tomb   waterfall

1   *castle*   2 _____   3 _____   4 _____

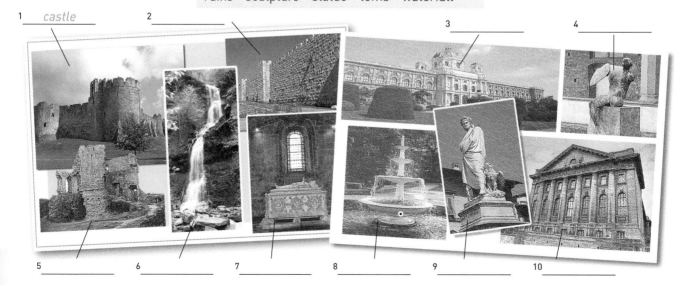

5 _____   6 _____   7 _____   8 _____   9 _____   10 _____

4 Complete the postcard using the correct past participle of the verbs in the box.

eat   meet   see   want

Hi!
Well, I've always ¹_____ to come here, and it's a beautiful place! We're having a great time – we've ²_____ all the sights and ³_____ some great food. And we've ⁴_____ some really nice people, too. Wish you were here!
Kirsten

Mark Edwards
43 Laurel Lane
Ashworth
Beds
HP9 4QQ

5 Complete the article using the questions in the box.

Over to you

Write your own answers to the six questions in Exercise 5.

a   What's the nicest hotel you've ever stayed in?
b   What's the most interesting place you've seen in your own country?
c   Have you had any bad experiences while travelling?
d   ~~What's the most beautiful place you've ever been to?~~
e   What's the strangest thing you've ever eaten when you're travelling?
f   Which country have you always wanted to visit?

My holidays

Michelle Giaquinto is from Australia. At the moment, she is working as a cook in a vegetarian restaurant in Italy. She has travelled to over 30 countries, including Mexico, Thailand, Nepal, Pakistan, Morocco, Guatemala, Turkey and many countries in Africa and Europe.

1 *What's the most beautiful place you've ever been to?*

It's difficult to choose the 'most beautiful' place I've visited, as every country has its personal bests. But I have very happy memories of the giant Himalayan mountains I walked through for three weeks in Nepal.

2 _____

I stayed in a beautiful little 'riad', or guesthouse, in Marrakech, Morocco. It wasn't very big, but it had a green courtyard with a fountain in the middle. The colourful tiles

everywhere gave it an exotic feel, too.

3 _____

The strangest thing I've tried were the fried crickets on the street in Bangkok, Thailand. You get three or four on a stick, and they're not bad – sweet and crunchy.

4 _____

I have always been very lucky in my travels, but someone stole my bag on a train when I

was in India. Getting very ill in a lonely part of Pakistan wasn't very nice, either.

5 _____

I still haven't visited Indonesia, a country with a very interesting culture and excellent diving sites to explore.

6 _____

Australia has so many interesting places to visit, as it's so large and diverse. But my favourites are the sights along the Great Barrier Reef, North Queensland. I also love the big, open spaces of our deserts and National Parks, especially Uluru National Park.

Present perfect
(*Have you
ever ... ?*)

6 Complete the questions using the past participle of the verbs in the box. Then complete the answers with *Yes* or *No*.

| be be eat ~~hear~~ hear see |

1 *Have you (ever) heard* of Machu Picchu?
  Yes , it's in Peru, I think.

2 _____ to New York?
  _____ , it's a fantastic city.

3 _____ Thai curry?
  _____ , I haven't. I don't really like spicy food.

4 _____ the Pyramids in Cairo?
  _____ , they're incredible!

5 _____ to France?
  _____ , but I've only been to Paris. What's the rest of the country like?

6 _____ of Uluru National Park?
  _____ , I have, but I've never been there.

Over to you

Write your own answers to the questions in Exercise 6.

MYEnglish

7 Read what Piet says and answer the questions.

1 Where does Piet work?
2 Why does he use English at work?
3 What two problems does he say he has with English?

" I work in the international department of a large bank in The Hague. I have a lot of colleagues who are not from my country, so I often use English at work. I learned English at school, of course, and when I was a student at university, I spent six months working for an international bank in Germany. That was a very good experience because the official language at work was English. I think my English is good now, but I know my pronunciation isn't perfect – I think the *th* sounds are very difficult. But I don't think this is a big problem – my colleagues understand me! One grammar mistake I often make is using the present perfect instead of the past simple, like *I have played tennis yesterday* instead of *I played tennis yesterday*. I think I need to practise more! "

Piet, Netherlands

Your English

8 Answer these questions.

1 Who do you use English with?
  • English-speaking people (from Britain, Ireland, the USA, Australia, etc.)
  • people from other countries?
2 Where do you use English?
  • in your country?
  • in English-speaking countries?
  • in other countries?

9 Do you have difficulty pronouncing *th* sounds? Go to the DVD-ROM for some practice.

EXPLORE Writing

10 Read these two extracts from a website where tourists write reviews of places they visit. Would you like to visit either of these places? Why? / Why not?

Address www.tripreviewer.com

Find the best things to do

Museum of Archaeology and Prehistory

Rating: ◉◉◉◉○

This is one of the most interesting museums in the town. It is in the centre, on the north side of the main square.

It has impressive Roman and Egyptian collections, and objects from Africa, Asia and Peru. In the Prehistory section, there are life-size models of dinosaurs.

The museum is open every day except Monday, from 10.00 am to 6.00 pm.

Adults €4.60 Under 16 €2.

Royal Gardens

Rating: ◉◉◉◉○

This is the town's biggest open space and the best place to go for some fresh air. The number 13 bus goes past it, or you can walk from the centre in 15 minutes.

The park has a café, a children's play area and a small lake, where you can rent a boat. And there's lots of grass to sit or lie on, or play Frisbee, football or cricket.

Open from 7.00 am to 7.00 pm. In summer, the park is open late and there's live music every evening.

---

11 Which text(s) includes this information? Write M (museum) and/or P (park).

1 where it is   M ☐
2 how to get there ☐ ☐
3 what you can see there ☐ ☐
4 what activities you can do there ☐ ☐
5 opening days/times ☐ ☐
6 ticket prices ☐ ☐

12 Complete these superlative expressions from the extracts in Exercise 10.

1 This is _____ _____ _____ most interesting museums in the town.

2 This is the town's _____ open space ...

3 ... and the _____ _____ to go for some fresh air.

13 Circle the correct words.

1 It has / is impressive Roman and Egyptian collections.
2 There / They are life-size models.
3 The park has / is a café.
4 There is / are lots of grass.
5 There / It is live music.

14 Complete the phrases with the correct prepositions, according to the websites.

1 It is _____ the centre, ...
2 _____ the north side _____ the main square.
3 The number 13 bus goes _____ it, ...
4 ... or you can walk _____ the centre _____ 15 minutes.

15 Correct these lists of things. Use commas (,) and write *and* where necessary.

1 objects from Africa Asia Peru
2 The park has a café a children's play area a small lake.

Look at the texts again to check.

16 Think of two places/things in your town/area that would be interesting for visitors. Think about what information you want to include (look at the list in Exercise 11) and write your recommendations.

1   Before you watch, look at part of the VSO website. VSO is a charity organisation that works in developing countries. Do you know other, similar organisations? Is there a similar organisation in your country?

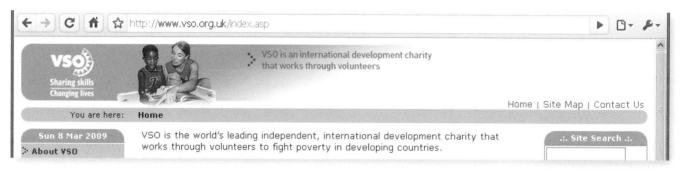

2   Watch parts 1 and 2 of the video. Choose the best summary of what Patrizia says.

Patrizia

a   Patrizia did voluntary work in Vietnam. She enjoyed the experience and now she would like to go to work in Africa.
b   Patrizia went on holiday to Vietnam. She enjoyed the experience, so she went to work in Africa as a marketing and communications officer.

3   Watch part 1 again (00:11–01:07). Tick (✓) the things in the advertisement that Patrizia mentions about her time with VSO.

> **Voluntary Service Overseas**
>
> ❂ working with local colleagues   ☑
> ❂ sharing professional skills   ☐
> ❂ cultural experiences   ☐
> ❂ learning new languages   ☐
> ❂ an insight into working abroad   ☐
> ❂ interesting travel   ☐

4   Watch part 2 again (01:07–01:58) and circle the correct answers.

1   Patrizia would like to work in Africa / Asia.
2   She would like to use her medical / marketing and communication skills
3   She went to Ethiopia for work / a holiday.
4   She really enjoyed / didn't enjoy her time in Ethiopia.

5   Look at the different ways Patrizia talks about work. Watch again and complete the sentences.

```
1                    … the opportunity to work ___alongside___ local colleagues, and this …
2               … have an insight into working_____ a foreign country, a very …
3         … and given me the desire to work _____, and this has now …
4      … my main ambition, and that is to work _____ an international development organisation.
5             … where I would like to work is _____ a country in Africa where …
6  … marketing and communication skills, possibly to work _____ a health organisation.
7       … given me the motivation to go and work _____ Africa and maybe in a different …
```

6   Would you like to do something like VSO? Explain why / why not.

GLOSSARY

volunteer (noun): a person who does something to help people – usually without being paid
insight (noun): the ability to understand what something is like
ambition (noun): something you really want to do in the future
international development (noun): projects to help improve the quality of life in countries around the world
diversity (noun): when many different types of thing or people are included in something
motivation (noun): your need or reason for doing something

14 Choices

1 Read the questionnaire and (circle) the answers that are most true for you.

Is your lifestyle good for you?

1 How much coffee or tea do you drink a day?

A none   **B** between one and three cups   **C** more than three cups

2 How much exercise do you do?

A 30–60 minutes every day   **B** 30–60 minutes a week   **C** none

3 How many hours do you sleep?

A 6–8 hours a night   **B** 8–11 hours a night   **C** 3–4 hours a night

4 How much water do you drink?

A more than one litre a day   **B** less than one litre a day   **C** none

5 How many hours do you work?

A 20–35 hours a week   **B** 35–40 hours a week   **C** 50–60 hours a week

6 How often do you eat fast food or sweets?

A never   **B** fewer than four times a week   **C** more than four times a week

7 How often do you eat fish?

A more than two times a week   **B** fewer than two times a week   **C** never

2 Complete the profiles. Write *too much*, *enough* or *not enough*.

Your profile:

IF YOU CHOSE MOSTLY A

You have a very good lifestyle. You get ¹ *enough* sleep and exercise, and you don't have ² _____ junk food or coffee. You drink ³ _____ water and you eat ⁴ _____ fish.

IF YOU CHOSE MOSTLY B

Your lifestyle is OK. Try to do more exercise and stop eating fast food and sweets!

IF YOU CHOSE MOSTLY C

Your lifestyle is not very good for you. You have ⁵ _____ work and ⁶ _____ sleep. You don't drink ⁷ _____ water or eat ⁸ _____ fish. You eat ⁹ _____ junk food.

Over to you

Look at your
questionnaire
answers and write
your profile.
My lifestyle is quite
good. I eat ...

VOCABULARY
Life changes

3 Complete the text about the changes in Anneke's life using the past simple of the verbs in the box.

> eat   get   get   get   go   have   have   ~~leave~~   move   start   take up

The choices I made

Anneke Kliegel, Switzerland, writes about the changes in her life and her hopes for the future.

" I ¹ _left_ school when I was 16 and I ² _____ a job in a fast-food café. I ³ _____ married to a lorry driver when I was 18 and ⁴ _____ a baby when I was 19. I had a very unhealthy lifestyle – I ⁵ _____ lots of junk food and didn't do any exercise, and I didn't use my brain. Then I ⁶ _____ divorced from my husband and decided to change my life. I became a vegetarian and ⁷ _____ yoga. I ⁸ _____ to India for two years, where I ⁹ _____ lessons in yoga and meditation. When I ¹⁰ _____ back to Switzerland three years ago, I ¹¹ _____ teaching yoga and stress management. I'm a much happier person now, and my daughter, Prisca, is happier, too.

In the future? I'm going to spend three months in India next summer, and I'm hoping to open my own yoga centre in a few years. And I'd like to have another child, a brother or sister for Prisca. "

GRAMMAR
be going to,
hoping to, would
like to

4 Look at these people's hopes and plans for the future. Write *'m, 'd* or *to* in the correct place.

I ᵐ hoping to go to university next year.

1 Thom

I'm going study in the States for six months.

2 Gemma

I'm hoping get married in the future.

3 Katrina

I like to take up a new sport, but I don't have time at the moment.

4 Kareem

I going to start a new job next month.

5 Anne-Marie

I'd like have children in the future.

6 Javier

Over to you

Write three sentences about your hopes and plans. Use *I'm going to ...*, *I'm hoping to ...* and *I'd like to.*

5 Who is more certain of his/her plans?

1   Thom or Gemma?
2   Anne-Marie or Javier?

VOCABULARY
Planning

6 Luisa and Ruth are planning their holiday. Put the words in the correct order to complete the conversation.

LUISA OK, so [1] are / what / we / about / to / do / going _what are we going to do about_ our holiday this year? We need to start planning.

RUTH I don't know. [2] like / to / would / you / go / to / Where / ?
_____

LUISA Maybe somewhere like the north of Europe? Somewhere not too hot.

RUTH Good idea. When can you go? I can be free in June or July.
[3] think / it's / too / I / busy _____
in August. And [4] really / accommodation / is / expensive.
_____

LUISA June [5] looks / me / to / good. _____ I'm not
too busy then. What would you like to do when we're there?

RUTH [6] sightseeing / to / like / I'd / do / some _____
and maybe relax, too.

LUISA Yeah, OK. Fine. Let's look at some websites this afternoon.

Time**Out**

7 Exercise your brain! Can you do these puzzles?

1 What's the missing letter?
J ? M A M J J A S O N D

2 Which is bigger: half of a quarter or a quarter of a half?

3 Cross out six letters. What word is left?
B S A I N X L E A T N T E A R S

4 What do an island and the letter T have in common?

5 What goes around the world but stays in a corner?

6 Put the letters in the right order. What do the words have in common?
T A R C O R   O O N I N   E T L E C T U   O T A O T P   C O B C R O I L

7 You have 50 spiders. How many legs and eyes do you have?

8 Write the two signs of the zodiac that contain these letters: COR

9 This sentense has two mistakes. What are they?

10 Some months have 30 days, some have 31. How many months have 28 days?

EXPLORE Reading

8 Read the web page on short holidays on page 79 and find the information.

1 Which holiday is the shortest? **C**
2 Which holiday is the longest? ☐
3 Which holiday is the most expensive? ☐
4 Which holidays can you NOT go on all year? ☐ ☐ ☐
5 Which holidays include flights from the UK? ☐ ☐
6 Which holidays can you ask for specially? ☐ ☐

9 Are these sentences about the holidays true or false?

1 You can see mountains and the sea on holiday A.   TRUE / FALSE
2 You only stay in bed and breakfasts on holiday B.   TRUE / FALSE
3 You don't stay in a hotel on holiday C.   TRUE / FALSE
4 You stay in a city on holiday D.   TRUE / FALSE
5 You stay in different places on holiday E.   TRUE / FALSE
6 You travel on a bus on holiday F.   TRUE / FALSE

10 Choose a holiday for each of these people.

1 Daniel is 28. He likes sports and nature and would like to visit the UK. He wants to go on holiday in May or June.
Holiday ☐
2 Jess and Colin are a couple. He likes nature and animals. She enjoys going to the gym and relaxing. They live in the UK.
Holiday ☐
3 Melanie and Serena are students. They want a sightseeing holiday that includes historical and natural sights. They would like to travel with a group.
Holiday ☐
4 Ulrike is 43 and single. She can only have three or four days' holiday and wants to relax. She would like to meet the local people in the country she visits.
Holiday ☐

11 Choose a holiday for Luisa and Ruth (see Exercise 6).

12 The web page asks people to review holidays they have been on. Look at what Kate Heneghan says and match the questions below (a–d) to her answers (1–4).

Read travellers' reviews

Reviewed 28 November by Kate Heneghan ★★★★★

1 It's difficult to say – the first sight of Petra, the crusader castle, sleeping under the stars … and how could I not mention the camel ride into the desert!

2 Book, go. Open your mind. Prepare to be amazed. Drink lots of bottled water. And take the minimum luggage needed.

3 The guides and drivers were all local, and the hotels were independently owned. We travelled as a group, so that cut down on petrol usage. We also travelled on specified routes through the Wadi Rum, so as not to disturb the nature, and they ensure there are rubbish facilities to keep the spaces clean.

4 Absolutely fantastic. It felt like a dream.

a ☐ How would you rate your holiday overall?
b ☐ What was the most memorable or exciting part of your holiday?
c ☐ Did you feel that your holiday benefited local people and minimised impacts on the environment?
d ☐ What tips would you give other travellers booking this holiday?

Over to you

Choose one of the holidays for you! Say where you would like to go and when.

13 Which holiday did Kate go on?

14 Answer the questions in Exercise 12 about a holiday you've been on.

www.short-breakholiday.com

Short-break holidays

Choose an original short-break holiday idea, weekend getaway, romantic short break or short-break adventure from specialist, responsible tour companies. All our short-break holidays are from the UK.

Ⓐ Orca watching in Norway

in brief: North of the Arctic Circle are the Lofoten Islands. In November, when the days are short, and the Northern Lights often shine over the snow-covered mountains, this is one of the best places in the world to see these beautiful whales.

type of trip: Small group, November

price: From €990 (4 days) excl. flights

Ⓑ Cycling holidays in England

in brief: A range of cycling breaks for people who want to explore England's countryside by bike. Accommodation in bed and breakfasts or small, family hotels.

type of trip: Small group, April–October

price: €265–€440 (3–5 days) excl. flights

Ⓒ Provence cooking and walking holidays

in brief: Live with the local people and meet their friends in rural France, cook and eat regional products, see the beautiful countryside and experience French culture from the inside.

type of trip: All year on request

price: From €430 (2 days), excl. flights

Ⓓ Birdwatching short break to Hungary

in brief: On the south slopes of the Bukk National Park in Eastern Hungary, Eger is the perfect place to see Hungary's spectacular bird life. Stay in a hotel with sauna, massage and fitness room.

type of trip: Small group, January–October

price: €285 (4 days), incl. UK flights

Ⓔ Short break to St Petersburg, Helsinki and Tallinn

in brief: Enjoy three classic cities of the Finnish Gulf. Travel by local transport, stay in central hotels, see the most important sights, and meet local people.

type of trip: All year on request

price: From €750 (6 days), excl. flights

Ⓕ Petra and Wadi Rum: short break to Jordan

in brief: From the capital, Amman, explore the hills and rocks of Wadi Rum valley by 4WD. Includes a visit to Kerak castle. Sleep in a Bedouin-style camp, then go to Petra, the ancient, rose-red city.

type of trip: Small group, all year

price: From €875 (5 days), incl. UK flights

1   Before you watch, match the activities (1–3) with the photos (a–c).

1   parachuting ☐   2   teaching English ☐   3   making radio programmes ☐

2   Watch Mainda, Salvatore and Leo talking about what they are hoping to do in the future. Who talks about each activity? Write M (Mainda), S (Salvatore) or L (Leo).

1   parachuting ☐   2   teaching English ☐   3   making radio programmes ☐

3 **a** Watch Mainda again (00:10–00:52). First tick (✓) the topics that she mentions.

health ☐   child care ☐   education ☐   work ☐

b Now tick (✓) the training she has done.

getting information for the programme ☐   using music ☐
structuring the programme ☐   presenting the programme ☐
working with sound ☐   asking good questions ☐

Mainda

4   Watch Salvatore again (00:53–01:20) and (circle) the correct answers.

1   Salvatore has always wanted / decided recently to do a parachute jump.
2   He thinks it's frightening / exciting to see the world under you.
3   He is planning to do a solo jump / jump with an instructor.

5   Watch Leo again (01:21–02:06). Complete the text about his work and studies using the words in the box.

classroom   learned   opportunities   teach   training   university   ~~work~~

Leo started ¹___work___ as an English language teacher and later received full
²_____ and education from a ³_____ in the UK. He would like to use
what he has ⁴_____ at university in the ⁵_____ . He also thinks teaching
English as a foreign language gives teachers ⁶_____ to travel round the world.
He would love to ⁷_____ in Cambodia.

Salvatore

Leo

6   Can you remember what the people say? Match the beginnings and endings of the sentences. Watch the video again to help you.

Mainda
1   I am hoping to ...
Salvatore
2   I'm planning to ...
Leo
3   I would like to ...
4   I would really love to ...

a   teach English.
b   work at my community radio station.
c   do it.
d   apply what I've learned.

7   Describe something you hope to do in the future. Try to use some expressions from Exercise 6.

GLOSSARY

issues (plural noun): important subjects or problems that people are discussing
and so forth (expression): an expression that means *and things like that* or *etc*.
gather (information) (verb): to find and collect (information)
apply /əˈplaɪ/ (verb): to use something in a practical situation
in tandem (expression): If you do something **in tandem**, you do it at the same time as another person.

Unit 8

1 2 twins 3 dad 4 mum 5 grandfather 6 grandmother
7 children 8 aunt 9 nephew 10 niece

2 2 funny 3 hard-working 4 creative 5 adventurous

3 2 pale 3 hair 4 brown 5 wearing 6 jacket

4 2 've got 3 Have you got 4 haven't got 5 hasn't got 6 Has

5 2 's got 3 hasn't got 4 hasn't got 5 have; got

6 2 get 3 talk 4 get 5 like 6 spend 7 know 8 are

7 2 C 3 C 4 NC 5 C 6 C 7 NC 8 C

8 wife, cousin, son, grandmother, dad, parents, uncle, twin(s),
children, niece, mum, nephew, grandfather, husband, daughter

9 1 False 2 False 3 True

10 2 a 3 b 4 c 5 d

11 1 designer 2 rock and folk 3 surfing 4 cold

DVD-ROM Extra

3 1 Nilgun 2 Leo 3 Hitin

4 2 His sisters give him 3 look 4 knows 5 two years 6 phone

5 2 love 3 close 4 young 5 call; make sure 6 visit
7 in touch 8 mum and dad

Unit 9

1 2 I cycle 3 I get a taxi 4 I drive 5 I get the bus
6 I ride a motorbike

2 2 do you know 3 best way 4 near here 5 take

3 2 What's the best way to get there? 3 Is it far?
4 How long does it take to walk?
5 And do you know what time it opens?

4 2 busier 3 more dangerous 4 the quickest
5 more interesting 6 the easiest

6 2 Departure 3 From 4 Direct 5 Price

7 1 Excuse me, how long does it take to get to London?
2 And how much does an open return cost, please?
3 OK, and is it direct?
4 What time does the next train leave?

8 1 False 2 True 3 True

10 2 slowly 3 dangerous 4 busy 5 expensive

12 2 a 3 c 4 b 5 a 6 b

13 Map A

14 1 The bus stop (Bus 128) is nearer
It's easier to come by bus or metro.
2 The nearest metro station is Priory Road.
The nearest car park is in Smithfield Street.

DVD-ROM Extra

2 learning English, dolphins, kangaroos, pizza, Sydney, trucks

3 1 18 2 France 3 years 4 couldn't understand anything
5 months

4 Picture 1

5 4, 2, 5, 1, 3

6 1 c 2 a 3 b

Unit 10

1 2 funny; laugh 3 scary; horrible 4 serious 5 love
6 an exciting; a lot 7 real 8 future

2 2 We could get 3 That sounds good 4 I'm not sure
5 Why don't we rent a DVD 6 Fine with me

3 2 are/'re coming 3 am/'m flying 4 are/'re going
5 is/'s arriving 6 am/'m coming back
7 are/'re waiting 8 isn't/is not working

4 2 F 3 F 4 F 5 N 6 F 7 N 8 N

5 2 – 3 – 4 on 5 – 6 – 7 at 8 in

6 2 ✓ 3 ✓ 4 She's speaking to Giulia on Friday morning. 5 ✓
6 ✓ 7 She's going to the cinema (with Paul) on Friday evening.
8 She's meeting Zhen at the airport on Saturday.

7 2 directed by 3 set in 4 it's about 5 character 6 stars
7 funny

8 See answers on page 57.

9 Classical music, Film, Children's events, Jazz, Walks, Rock music

10 1 False 2 True 3 True 4 False

11 1 Scandellara Festival (Jurassic Rock) 2 City Walks
3 Kids' Summer (Clowns) 4 Open-air jazz

DVD-ROM Extra

2 2 H 3 A 4 A 5 H

3 1 b 2 a 3 b

4 2 fun 3 love story 4 happy 5 songs 6 family 7 friends

5 1 d 2 c 3 b 4 a

Unit 11

1 2 check in 3 boarding gate 4 baggage drop
5 baggage reclaim 6 customs 7 passport control

2 2 belt 3 passport 4 pack 5 laptop 6 gate 7 keys 8 bag
9 anything

3 2 S 3 C 4 C 5 S 6 C 7 S 8 S 9 C

4 a 3 b 2 c 5 d 1 e 4

5 a 2,8 b 3,10 c 4,7 d 1 e 6,9 f 5

6 2 at the time 3 the south of 4 I was with 5 and then
6 in the middle of 7 In the end 8 It was quite frightening

7 2 waited 3 shopping 4 checked 5 cancelled 6 wanted
7 delayed 8 started 9 checked 10 delayed

8 1 a little 2 reading

9 4, 5, 8

11 2 understand 3 spell 4 how much
5 slow down 6 which

12 2 the travel company 3 Greece 4 delayed
5 an apology and some money

13 a 3 b 1 c 2

14 2 free seats 3 to complain 4 to receive 5 was delayed
6 satisfied 7 some compensation

15 1 Dear Sir or Madam 2 I am writing to …
3 I look forward to your reply 4 Yours faithfully

DVD-ROM Extra

2 Croatia and the USA

3 2 similar 3 meaning 4 some trousers 5 'year' 6 helicopter
7 front 8 glass 9 a couple of hours

4 1 excited; confident 2 offended 3 amazing

Unit 12

1 2 throat 3 mouth 4 back 5 arm 6 elbow 7 wrist
8 shoulder 9 finger 10 leg 11 knee 12 ankle

2 2 sore throat 3 every four to six hours 4 children under 12
5 WARNING! 6 allergic to 7 Keep away from

3 2 should (G) 3 should (L) 4 Get (L) 5 should (G) 6 Take (G)
7 shouldn't (L) 8 Don't listen (G)

5 2 a 3 d 4 b 5 e 6 c

6 have a meeting, have a party, have fun, have lunch
take a train, take tablets
spend money, spend time

7 2 take a train 3 have fun 4 have a meeting 5 spend; time

8

L	Q	Z	E	W	Y	W	T	U	S	P	I	G	S	M
Y	K	Y	U	B	F	U	H	R	S	N	A	D	Q	D
E	T	I	V	O	Z	T	R	U	M	K	Z	L	T	Q
N	E	C	K	H	N	O	O	Z	F	C	I	R	L	N
C	S	V	I	E	Q	E	A	E	U	T	L	N	J	U
C	T	M	Y	A	B	G	T	K	U	S	A	B	K	T
T	O	U	G	D	Y	Z	Y	Z	N	E	E	A	O	F
F	M	S	P	O	V	P	Q	N	I	E	W	C	D	A
D	A	C	B	U	O	K	S	X	M	S	E	K	K	C
T	C	L	H	E	S	Y	R	F	I	N	G	E	R	E
G	H	E	E	A	N	K	L	E	W	J	R	A	P	F
F	U	F	H	J	L	S	M	V	X	H	E	Z	S	N
G	L	B	N	M	U	F	O	O	T	V	Y	K	V	X
Y	J	E	M	O	U	T	H	I	L	M	L	C	L	O
I	Q	M	G	P	C	H	S	H	O	U	L	D	E	R

9 A 1 B 3 C 2
10 4 a 8 c 12 b
11 b 8 c 11 d 10 e 5 f 1
12 b ✗ c ✓ d ✗ e ✗ f ✓

DVD-ROM Extra

2 1 sleep 2 exercise 3 food and diet 4 medicine
3 2 boring 3 a couple of times 4 brown; wholemeal
  5 buys organic food 6 Ayurvedic
4 1 b iii 2 c ii 3 a i
5 2 a 3 d 4 f 5 b

Unit 13

1 2 i 3 b 4 l 5 d, (f) 6 j 7 k 8 a 9 e/j/l 10 b/c/i/l
  11 a/f/g/i 12 b/h/i/l
2

	Verb	Past participle
Regular verbs (–ed)	use	used
	smoke	smoked
	play	played
	work	worked
	like	liked
	want	wanted
Irregular	meet	met
	eat	eaten
	be	been
	read	read
	have	had
	see	seen

3 2 city walls 3 palace 4 sculpture 5 ruins 6 waterfall
  7 tomb 8 fountain 9 statue 10 museum
4 1 wanted 2 seen 3 eaten 4 met
5 2 a 3 e 4 c 5 f 6 b
6 2 Have you (ever) been to New York?
  Yes, it's a fantastic city.
  3 Have you (ever) eaten Thai curry?
  No, I haven't. I don't really like spicy food.
  4 Have you (ever) seen the Pyramids in Cairo?
  Yes, they're incredible!
  5 Have you (ever) been to France?
  Yes, but I've only been to Paris. What's the rest of
  the country like?
  6 Have you (ever) heard of Uluru National Park?
  Yes, I have, but I've never been there.

7 1 In the international department of a bank in The Hague.
  2 He has a lot of colleagues who are not from his country.
  3 He finds it hard to pronounce the *th* sound. He uses the present
  perfect instead of the past simple.
11 2 P 3 M/P 4 P 5 M/P 6 M
12 1 one of the 2 biggest 3 best place
13 2 There 3 has 4 is 5 There
14 1 in 2 on; of 3 past 4 from; in
15 1 objects from Africa, Asia and Peru
  2 The park has a café, a children's play area and a small lake.

DVD-ROM Extra

2 a
3 working with local colleagues, sharing professional skills, cultural
  experiences, an insight into working abroad
4 1 Africa 2 marketing and communication
  3 a holiday 4 really enjoyed
5 2 in 3 abroad 4 for 5 in 6 in 7 in

Unit 14

2 2 too much 3 enough 4 enough 5 too much 6 not enough
  7 enough 8 enough 9 too much
3 2 got 3 got 4 had 5 ate 6 got 7 took up 8 went 9 had
  10 moved 11 started
4 2 I'm going **to** study in the States for six months.
  3 I'm hoping **to** get married in the future.
  4 I**'d / would** like to take up a new sport …
  5 I**'m / am** going to start a new job next month.
  6 I'd like **to** have children in the future.
5 1 Gemma 2 Anne-Marie
6 2 Where would you like to go to?
  3 I think it's too busy
  4 accommodation is really expensive.
  5 looks good to me
  6 I'd like to do some sightseeing
7 1 F (They are the first letters of the months of the year.)
  2 They are the same: $\frac{1}{8}$
  3 BANANA (You cross out S-I-X L-E-T-T-E-R-S!)
  4 They are both in the middle of waTer.
  5 a stamp (It stays in the corner of the letter.)
  6 CARROT, ONION, LETTUCE, POTATO, BROCCOLI (They are all
  vegetables.)
  7 Two legs and two eyes – we didn't ask about the spiders!
  8 CapriCORn and SCORpio
  9 First mistake: the correct spelling is *sentence*.
  Second mistake: the sentence only has one mistake, not two!
  10 All of them!
8 2 E 3 A 4 A,B,D 5 D,F 6 C,E
9 2 False 3 True 4 False 5 True 6 False
10 1 B 2 D 3 F 4 C
11 Holiday E
12 a 4 b 1 c 3 d 2
13 Holiday F

DVD-ROM Extra

1 1 b 2 c 3 a
2 1 S 2 L 3 M
3 a) health, child care, work
  b) getting information for the programme, structuring the
  programme, working with sound, asking good questions
4 1 has always wanted 2 exciting 3 jump with an instructor
5 2 training 3 university 4 learned 5 classroom
  6 opportunities 7 teach
6 1 b 2 c 3 a 4 d

Acknowledgements

The authors would like to thank the editorial team in Cambridge, particularly Greg Sibley. Chris Cavey and Maggie Baigent would also like to thank Nick Robinson for his good humour, patience and ideas in his role as Project Manager in the earlier stages of the work. Many thanks also to Catriona Watson-Brown for her ever-thorough copy-editing.

Maggie Baigent would like to thank Michael Cotton for his loyalty and support.

Chris Cavey would like to thank Kate, Lily and Ella for their patience and support.

Nick Robinson would like to thank Anna Barnardo.

The authors and publishers are also grateful to the following contributors:

Design and page make-up: Stephanie White at Kamae Design
Picture research: Hilary Luckcock

The authors and publishers acknowledge the following sources of copyright material and are grateful for the permissions granted. While every effort has been made, it has not always been possible to identify the sources of all the material used, or to trace all copyright holders. If any omissions are brought to our notice, we will be happy to include the appropriate acknowledgements on reprinting.
Bell International for the extract on p12. Copyright © www.bell-centres.com/malta; Good Hope Studies for the extract on p12; Kirsty de Garis for the extract on p22, © Kirsty de Garis; Alice Fisher for the extract on p42. Copyright Guardian News & Media Ltd 2007; VSO, www.vso.org.uk, for the extract on p68.

The publisher has used its best endeavours to ensure that the URLs for external websites referred to in this book are correct and active at the time of going to press. However, the publisher has no responsibility for the websites and can make no guarantee that a site will remain live or that the content is or will remain appropriate.

The publishers are grateful to the following for the permissions to reproduce copyright photographs and material:

Key: l = left, c = centre, r = right, t = top, b = bottom

Alamy Images/©Jason Hosking for p4(b), /©Jason Hosking for p5(3), /Image Source Black for p5(bl), /©Radius Images for p5(br), /©Annette Price-H20 Photography for p6(cr), /©Ian Shaw for p6(br), /©Blend Images for p10, /©Cultura for p11(c), /©B L Images Ltd for p12(tl), /©S C Photos for p12(tc), /©Peter Treanor for p12(tr), /©Rubberball for p14(3), /©GoGo Images Corporation for p14(4), /©Profimedia International s.r.o. for p15, /©GlowImages for p16, /©North River Images for p19, /©David R Frazier Photolibrary Inc for p21, /©Westend61 for p26(r), /©Andrew Woodley for p29(t), /©GlowImages for p30, /©JupiterImages/Creatas for p34(tc), /©GlowImages for p34(bc), /©Blend Images for p34(br), /©Rohit Seth for p41, /©GoGoImages Corporation for p44(1), /©Uppercut Images for p44(2), /©Jim Powell for p44(3), /©Radius Images for p50(b), /©Robert Holmes for p53(t), /©Rubberball for p55(t), /©imagebroker for p55(ct), /©Buzzshotz for p55(cb), /©vario images GmbH & Co KG for p56(c), /©Adrian Lascom for p65(c), /©Phovoir/FCM Graphic for p65(bl), /©GoGo Images Corporation for p70(1), /©Rubberball for p70(3), /©Radius Images for p70(5), /Westend61 for p70(6) /©ImagesEurope for p73(tr); Corbis/©Wolf-zefa for p11(t), /©Darren Modricker for p27(l), /©Amanaimages for p46(tr), /©Image Source for p60(tl); Education Photos for pp34(bl), 44(4), 44(5), 44(b); Getty Images/©Iconica for p6(tl), /©GAB Archive/Redfern for p22(l), /©GAB Archive Redfern for p22(r), /© Harald Eisenberger for p24(b), /Harald Eisenberger for p26(l), /©Tom Bonaventure for p46(br), /©Daisuke Oka/Sebun Photo for p46(bl), /©Somos/Veer for p60(b), /©Larry Dale Gordon for p73(tc); Hannover Marketing & Tourismus GmbH for p24(c); istockphoto/©Jennifer London for p24(tr), /©G_studio for p34(tr), /©Byron W Moore for p45(t), /©James Cameron for p52, /©mseidlch for p55(b), /©Antonio D'Albore for p56(b), /©RainforestAustralia for p65(tr), /©sverx for p66(t), /©Contour99 for p70(2); Kobal Collection/©Lucas Film/Paramount Pictures for p49(r), /©RBT Stigwood Prods/Hemdale for p51(cl), /©MGM for p57(cr), /©Dreamworks for p51(b); Masterfile/©Norbert Schafer for p5(1), /©Artiga Photo for p5(2), /©John Gertz for p5(4), /©Tomas Rodriguez for p5(5), /©Tim Kuisalaas for p5(6), /©Norbert Schafer for p5(7), /©Kathleen Finlay for p5(8); Photolibrary/©PhotoDisc for p6(tr), /©PhotoDisc for p7, /©Cultura for p11(b), /©Uppercut Images for p14(2), /©Bananastock for p34(tl), /©Image Source for p36(r), /©Image Source for p37, /©PhotoDisc for p39(t), /©Uppercut Images for p44(6), /©Ambient Images for p45(b), /©imagebroker.net for p56(t), /©Image Source for p66(b), /©Radius Images for p70(4), /©Fancy for p70(t), /©Blend Images for p71, /©imagestate for p73(tl), /©F1 Online for p73(bl); Punchstock/©Valueline for p9, /©Digital Vision for p12(bl), /©Image Source for p14(1), /©Cultura for p14(5), /©PhotoAlto Agency for p14(6); Rex Features/©Sony Pics/Everett for p51(t); Ronald Grant Archive/©Dreamworks for p49(l); Shutterstock/©Jonathon Brizendine for p13(br), /©Leah-Anne Thompson for p24(tl), /©Denis Babenko for p27(r), /©maribell for p32(l), /©Robyn Mackenzie for p32(r), /©Sklep Spozywczy for p33(l), /©Joe Gough for p33(r), /©Thomas Sztanek for p36(l), /©Andrew Gentry for p58(b), /©Yuri Arcurs for p59(b), /©Imagery/Majestic for p60(tr), /©Galvia Barskaya for p61, /©Orange Line Media for p63(tl), /©Kiselev Andrey Valerevich for p63(tcl), /©Phase4Photography for p63(tcr), /©Olga Kushcheva for p63(tr), /©Andrei Nekrassov for p73(bc), /©Regien Paassen for p73(br); Tom Craig for p42; Topfoto for p40(b).

Illustrations by Tom Croft, Mark Duffin, Clare Elsom, Kamae Design, Julian Mosedale, Nigel Sanderson, Sean Simms, Lucy Truman

Notes